Pillars and Prophets:

Helping Western Christians understand the Muslim World

By Carl Medearis
with Phillip Strople

Copyright 2006 Carl Medearis

INTRODUCTION

WHY THIS BOOK?

Why read this book?

This book began almost twenty years ago. Back then, communism, the Cold War, and nuclear détente were nearing their decline. The Reagan administration was in it's second term, and the majority of the American population knew very little about the Middle East, Islam, or Islamic terrorism. Baath party-socialist Saddam Hussein had been in power for only six years, and the secular government of Iraq was in a constant state of war with Shi'ite neighbor, Iran. There was little to no fear or suspicion of Islam in the West, mainly because the reality of terrorism was not yet on our doorstep. In fact, most people knew nothing of Islam other than what they heard on the news: the Afghan campaign against Soviet troops, the Iran-Contra affair, and the Carter administration's failed rescue attempts in Tehran.

Libya's Muammar Khaddafi was a top-shelf bad guy.

The Ayatollah Khomeini had replaced the CIA-sponsored Shah of Iran, and oil prices were back down to "normal" after the oil scare of the late seventies. For the most part, all was quiet on the Middle-Eastern front.

The Western world, America, in particular, was unaware of the threat it would face in the future, and, as is the case in most peaceful times, knew next to nothing about the nature of the threat.

Until a few years ago.

As the West looked with sorrow and shock at the smoldering wreckage which spewed smoke and ash into the Manhattan sky, I was busy trying to console my friends and family in Beirut, Lebanon. My phone rang all day. One Muslim friend after another called me, each completely in shock. One friend in particular came by our house, sat on the couch opposite me, and rubbed his face with his hands. "Carl," he said, "these terrorists have just shattered the peace we have worked so hard for."

"What do you mean?" I asked.

"America will go to war," he said, shaking his head, "and I am afraid that it will not end for years."

"I know."

"The West does not understand us. They see an Arab, and they feel fear. They hear talk of Islam, and they are suspicious. I am afraid that things will spiral out of control, and that hatred will grow between my people and your people," he sighed, "again."

"Ahmed," (not his real name) I said, looking him in the eyes, "we are each other's people. We are both followers of Jesus, friends of God, and brothers in a way that boundaries cannot take from us."

"I know," he said, "but to see Islam and Christianity at war once again is something that will break my heart. I have so many loved ones on both sides." A tear slid down his face and he tried to wipe it away before I could see it.

I lived in Lebanon from 1992 until 2004, and I invested time into my friendships. If 9/11 was going to rip the world apart, I was going to do everything I could to stop it. We had worked long to build friendships and the last thing I wanted was to let them be torn away by international politics, hatred and misunderstanding.

3

During that time I made several trips into Iraq. The war in Iraq had torn the status quo up by the roots, and my Iraqi friends were practically pleading with us to come over.

It was ethereal, to say the least. We halted at a coalition checkpoint, and for the first time in years, I heard the Midwestern accent of an American in the middle of the desert. Welcome to Iraq; may I take your order? The troops were enthusiastic; GI's doing their job. We shook hands, exchanged pleasantries, and hit the road again, southbound for Basra.

A few weeks later, my life nearly ended, along with the rest of the team. As we returned North on the route at a hundred and sixty klicks per hour, we were overtaken by a black Mercedes with one notable distinction: rifles. We were forced to the shoulder, forced into the back seat, and escorted out into the sand, below the lip of a wadi, out of sight. Once again, we were dragged from our vehicle, lined up in the sand on our knees, hearts pounding, palms sweating.

Let me tell you: when the muzzle of an AK-47 stares you in the eye, you find an incredible capacity for introspection, along with a unique closeness to God.

I had to ask myself: *if I had to do it all over again, would I spend my life in the Middle East, living among Arabs, trying to be a visible expression of Jesus to them?*

I had my answer before I finished asking the question. Even while the barrel of a rifle was shoved in my face, I heard the Holy Spirit speak inside of me so strongly that I could feel my body tremble.

I love these people.

When I heard that, I realized the truth: I loved these Arabs, too. But it wasn't *my* love that drove me – it was His love for them. I was simply a part of the story.

Sadly, when we returned to the United States, we found that the temper of western Christianity was markedly different.

TV, radio, magazine articles, pulpit briefs: so many voices, so much conflict.

Some voices called for the complete destruction of Islamic nations, and even Islam on the whole. These opinions mostly came from politically motivated figures, but they were disturbing notwithstanding. Others disagreed with that position, but it seemed that almost no one knew what to do, what to say, or even what to hope for.

Politically, however, many religious voices found an outlet where they could iterate their political allegiances and use them to fire upon Muslims, Arabs, and even non-Christians et al.

Few did this with the poise of Jesus.

It is at this juncture that I came to a horrifying realization. The momentum within Christianity was moving rapidly into the realm of politics.

The problem was not justifiable national defense, but rather the lack of discernment, as Christians who felt wounded and vulnerable from the 9/11 attacks found it relatively easy to assume terrorism was synonymous with Islam, and therefore it became justifiable in the eyes of western Christianity to beat our plowshares back into swords. Some American Christians, who, understandably, were "all for war" in terms of patriotism and national defense, nevertheless reintroduced a problem which has not been seen since the crusades. Falsely aligning man's causes with God's causes, linking our military successes to his will, and broadcasting the message that God is "on our side."

At least that's how my Arab friends saw it. *The Christians are coming, again.*

I realize that this is a distinction which does not include all Westerners, Americans, or all Christians, either. I also realize that I am treading on sensitive ground with this subject. I am not saying that defense and security issues should be ignored.

I don't intend to speak for God into any kind of political venue. In fact, when I'm asked, as I often am, what is the answer to the issues in the Middle East, and I answer "Jesus" I am often mocked as being simplistic – even by friends who are committed Christians.

They are looking for a political answer that simply doesn't exist.

I am a reductionist. When I can't make sense of things, I pull everything back to it's simplest point, boiling away the confusion and noisy complexities. What matters is what has always mattered:

Jesus.

After relocating back to the United States, I received invitation after invitation to speak at universities, churches, and some events which just seemed to be a group of eager listeners in chairs without any particular sponsorship. I was puzzled by what I considered to be my newfound popularity. And one day, I realized the truth. It wasn't *me* that people were interested in, it was a thirst that had awakened in America, a desire to become more familiar with this religion called Islam. My ego wasn't deflated at all, in fact, the opposite – my heart surged with hope. Many Christians were choosing the road less traveled; driven to find out what Islam was like, and thirsty to see if there was a way to reach out to them with the compassion of Christ.

I cannot hope to speak for all sides of every issue. If there are components of this book which you disagree with, please do not be upset. Rather, realize that these are the suggestions of a man who has only his experiences to quote from. I'm not infallible, I'm not the final word on Islam. I'm only a follower of Jesus who loves Muslims. So, to answer the question we began with, maybe you're reading this book because you want to understand your Muslim friend or neighbor. Maybe you want to go to the Middle East to share Jesus' love with people. Maybe you're just curious about what makes a Muslim different from you. In any case, my intention is to give you some information to help you befriend a Muslim, and some practical tips on how to live a life that's truly good news to a Muslim. This book, is not, in any way intended to be the complete and final treatise on this issue.. Just helpful and genuine.

This book has two parts to each chapter. The first part of every chapter is devoted to a topic on what Muslims believe. My hope is to fairly represent them. I've had several Muslim scholars read each of these chapters and they have agreed that what I've said is "fair." The second half of each chapter is what I believe would be a response sanctioned by Jesus Christ. For those of us looking to live our lives as much like Jesus as possible — I attempt to lay out what He might want us to do with the subject at hand in that chapter.

"The grace of the Lord Jesus Christ, and the love of God, and the friendship of the Holy Spirit be with all of you." (2 Corinthians 13:14)

Carl Medearis, Denver 2006

1. BEFORE THE PILLARS

THE FOUNDATIONS OF ISLAM

The Prophet Muhammad

In the late sixth century AD, a boy was born in Mecca, Arabia. His father was already deceased, and his mother died when he was six. This boy would unite the Arab people, wage military campaigns, and become revered as a prophet to millions of people for over a millennia.

His name was Muhammad. He is one of the most memorable individuals in all of human history, and his name is synonymous with the modern personality of Islam. Outside of Islam and it's reach, Muhammad is held at arm's length in the interest of scrutiny and theology. Recent observations have shed much light on the person of Muhammad, his language, his culture, and his shaping. The latter is of primary importance to scholars, evangelists, and apologists who wish to either explain his ways or reject them. Regardless of this scholastic influx, it must be said that first and foremost, Muhammad was a leader of men. Even today, Islam is the fastest growing religion in the world, and Islam is the most revered-by-fear religion in the history of the three monotheisms: Judaism, Christianity, and Islam.

Not much is known of him before his fortieth year, but studies of the history of the period help fill in the gaps. Mecca was an important hub for trade routes and enterprise, and it is speculated that Muhammad was involved with commerce from an early age, taking business trips as far as Syria before he was fifteen.

Mecca was a through-route for caravans, and also held an important position in the maritime trades, providing a product and financial clearing house of sorts for both India and Africa.

Although Muslims regard the era of Muhammad's birth and childhood as the end of a time of ignorance, there was, without doubt, a platform of various religious beliefs, and a wide variety of practices. Christians had settled in many places in Arabia, and many Jews had settled comfortably in Arabia, for purposes of business and expansion.

The Arabs of the period were largely pantheistic, and many were outright idolatrous, worshipping a variety of deities and idols.

Nevertheless, the shrine of Mecca - *the Kaba* - was a recognized religious center for Arabs. The shrine was a haven for a series of sacred stones, the most important of which was the 'Black Stone' which came from heaven. The Black Stone is built into the eastern corner of the Kaba, and annual pilgrimages required the sojourners to come and approach the stone.

However, according to various sources, there may have been as many as three hundred deities worshipped at the Kaba.

At the time, Jewish and Christian cultures had a religious impact on the Arabs, which you will notice if you read through the Muslim holy book, the Qur'an. The Jews shared their folklore with their Arab neighbors, as did the Christians, spreading at least a superficial understanding of the religion of the one God and the man Jesus. Many of the stories you can read in the Old and New Testaments are easily found, at least in part, in the Qur'an.

Although nothing was recorded about Muhammad until over a century after his death, the Muslim traditions have some light to shed on him. He was raised by his uncle and the tribe of his family, the Quraysh, who were, at the time responsible for the care of the Kaba, and the influence of religion began during his earliest years.

According to legend, while he was in a caravan on a business trip, he met with a Nestorian monk. The Nestorians were heretic Christians, having been officially declared outside the church in the mid-fifth century.

This monk believed that Muhammad was a prophet, and supposedly told him so.

Later on, Muhammad became quite a prominent businessman, a member of the guild at Mecca, as well as a prolific traveler. He traded stories and discussions about God and religion with many Jews and Christians, fervently absorbing as much information as he could.

While the modern west typically paints Muhammad as a false prophet intent on misleading people, it is important that we consider that Muhammad was at least in the beginning, a man with a desire to discover God. As he circuited Arabia, discussing God with the Christians and the Jews and the pantheistic and idolatrous Arabs, it is easy to see how he became disillusioned with the likenesses of God that were available to him.

Muhammad married an important woman who was fifteen years older than he was, and because she was wealthy and well connected to the trades, Muhammad became a man of importance by managing her caravan. Her name was Khadijah, and they had seven children together, six of whom died young. After Khadijah passed on, some twenty-plus years later, Muhammad married a dozen or more women.

At the age of forty, Muhammad became more and more concerned with the sacrilegious practices around him. He felt that mankind was straying from the path of God, that people were diluting the truth and falling away from true religion.

According to tradition, Muhammad found a cave on Mt. Hirah, not far from Mecca, and he used the solitude of the place to meditate. It was during these meditations that he heard the voice of God, or, as some believe, the messenger of God, Gabriel the Archangel (Jibrail).

Muhammad was given a series of messages which he believed were from God; he also believed that he was meant to give them to others. These messages were compiled some time after his death, and formed into the Qur'an.

Muhammad was not popular at first. In fact, the vast majority of Mecca wanted nothing to do with him. His message was extreme, and he promised that God would judge those who did not listen and obey. Because he was vocal about the primacy of the One God, he was considered a threat to the Kaba and the business around it, many of which thrived on the business of the city's religious culture.

Those who followed Muhammad's teaching were called *Muslim*, which means, literally, "submitted to God."

From the beginning, there was persecution. The people of Mecca were violent, and their aggression was condoned by the leadership of the city, and before long, Muhammad and his family of believers moved to the Christian kingdom of Abyssinia. They settled in a city called Yathrib (later renamed Medina), where the people were more open to hear the teachings of this new prophet. At first, both Christians and Jews were actually quite receptive to the message of Muhammad, mainly because he was adamant about the

11

sovereignty of one true God, and that worshipping other gods would bring judgment and wrath.

It is at this point in history where *Islam*, meaning "surrender" or "submission," transitioned from a family-sized cell into the beginnings of an actual religious movement. The Muslim calendar began in 622. The subsequent military campaigns allowed the participants of warfare to receive compensation for their work, and Muhammad utilized this to form a more cohesive body out of his following. There were seventy-six of these battles during Muhammad's lifetime.

Christianity and Judaism were at first of no consequence to Muhammad. In fact, Muhammad is known to have preached and supported the veracity of the claims of the Torah, the Jewish prophets, and the teachings of Jesus. But over time, it became clear that Muhammad was a different sort of prophet altogether, and so the Jews failed to hold him in the esteem he desired, and because the Christians already had prophets, apostles, and a messiah, Muhammad didn't fit. After some time Muhammad found himself speaking primarily to his Arabic countrymen.

By the time of his death, in 632, Muhammad had unified the Arab people, he had provided them with teaching, codified law, and he had given them military victories. By the 730's Islam had spread as far as Spain and France. Syria, Iraq, Egypt, Persia (Iran), Afghanistan, all of North Africa (now Libya, Algeria, Morocco) all fell to Islam.

While we're discussing the beginning, I think there are some important things to point out. Muhammad never had any intention of starting a *new* religion. He did not consider Islam to be his creation, rather he considered Islam to be the call to return to the one true God - the God of Abraham - to submit to Allah.

It is vitally important to know what the word *Allah* means. *Allah* is Arabic for "God." This must be said, as many people believe that Allah is the *name* of *a* god whom Muslims worship. The word *Allah* was used by Arab Christians during Muhammad's time. In fact, Christians in the Arab world, even as you read this, pray to *Allah* every day. They're praying to God.

It is important to be clear about this since there are numerous people who believe that Allah is the pagan god of the moon or the sun. When any true believer prays in Arabic, God *is* Allah, and Allah *is* God. In fact, every translation of the Bible into Arabic uses the word Allah for God.

There are some who disagree, and it is their contention that the word "Allah" comes from a pre-Islamic name for a moon-god. The word may have connotations from earlier usage, but even if this is so, those meanings have long lost since their definitive quality. Allah comes from an Arabic root *Al-Ilah*, which simply means "the god," or "the deity."

Allah is linguistically related to the Hebrew word "Elohim" and is also related to the Aramaic "Elo" and "Alaah" In the time of Christ, the word used for "God" was linguistically closer to the Arabic word than it was to the pagan Germanic word that we now use, which is "God."

A Christ-like perspective

Know the message
The most important thing we can do as followers of Jesus is to do just that. Follow him. Remember, Jesus has all authority in heaven and on earth, and it is he himself who is the gospel. The message that we carry is Jesus. Not church,

not capitalism, not democracy, not doctrine, not the religion of Christianity, not Calvin, not Luther, not Clinton, not Bush.

If we truly wish to be able to build a relationship with a Muslim friend, the most important thing we can do is to follow Jesus' lead. Jesus had compassion for people, and he valued the same quality in his disciples, even above personal sacrifice.

If we begin our mission with the attitude that we are going to debunk "all of that Islamic stuff" we'll be done before we get a chance to introduce Jesus, and we will have offended somebody in the process.

Some suggestions:

Don't insult Muhammad, and don't be flippant with religious phrases or with God or your bible. Show respect, and you may well be respected for it.

Do everything you can to keep it from becoming a *me-versus-you* debate. That's not what Jesus was about, we would do well to follow his example.

Show interest in your Muslim friends' faith. Not as a means of deception, but because they are your friend, and because you are interested in them and what they think about God. In fact, keeping the conversation on common ground and everyday spirituality will prove to be far more effective than apologetics and confrontation. Many Muslims are uneducated regarding their religion, and any attempt to force a theological point will end in shared frustration. One thing you will notice about Arab Muslims in particular is that the Arabic sense of logic is totally different than ours.

For example: when I first arrived in Beirut, I attempted to use C.S. Lewis' tried-and-true "Liar, Lord, or Lunatic" approach with my new friends. I said that because Jesus himself claimed to be the way, truth and life that this was either true or not. Jesus was either who he said he was, or he was lying about it, or even worse, he was delusional. Those were the only options.

"No," they said, shaking their heads. "He was a prophet of God, and he never told lies and he certainly wasn't crazy."

"Don't you see," I would plead, "the only option left is that he is Lord?"

"No. He was something else. You need more options in your argument."

"There *aren't any,*" I said, palms sweaty. "I'm being logical, and Jesus was logical."

That raised some eyebrows.

Only later did I realize that they had raised an interesting point: Jesus lived in their region, spoke a similar language, had similar ethnic qualities.

And then Carl the Great White Missionary flew across the world to tell them that Jesus was logical...like an American.

Be genuine, and be patient. Whatever denomination or church we come from, it is not our job to "secure converts." In bolder terms, we are not even there to "build the kingdom," but rather to obey the king. Kings build their own kingdoms and Jesus surely can build his. We are involved in the process because we follow Him.

One other note about Jesus: use his title as a term of respect, i.e. "Jesus the Christ" (or Messiah), this is actually a term that Muslims accept, and it shows a sense of reverence.

Many Muslims are surprised when they see a westerner praying, reading a Bible, or treating religious things with a sense of devotion. This is because we in the west are used to the "separation of church and state," and so we are acclimated to the non-religious norms within our culture. Muslims see this as a blatant disregard of devotion to God. Many of my Muslim friends are surprised when I tell them that the president or some public figure believes in God. They don't see it in the media, where talk of God is rare, and devotion toward him seems nonexistent. Within Islamic nation-states, the opposite is true. Every Islamic state, (even the secular ones) is permeated with religious devotion and/or tradition. Every public figure is a Muslim. Every political office carries with it some influence of Islamic law, to one degree or another.

We don't want to wear our devotion on our sleeve, but we do want to truly be people of the Spirit; people who are obviously seeking to follow the ways of God and be more like Jesus. This really is what we desire and it will pave the way for many genuine friendships.

11. THE TEACHINGS OF ISLAM

PILLARS AND PROPHESIES

The basic principles

Muslims are obliged to acknowledge certain articles of faith, known as *Iman;* objects or doctrine. According to Islam, there are several absolutes, which every good Muslim must confess with his tongue and believe in his heart. The form in which this is pronounced goes like this: "I believe in God , his angels, his books, his prophets, in the last day," [and some add] "in the predestination by the Most High God of good and evil, and in the resurrection after death."

On the whole there's really nothing disagreeable about anything in this statement. In fact, it's similar to a churches' statement of faith, in almost every way.

The Bible places a high value on many of the same articles. Where is the difference?   In   a   side-by-side comparison with the Bible, the Muslim statement of faith is missing one primary thing.

Jesus.

The primary thing that we have to offer to our Muslim friends is Jesus. That's who we need. That's who they need.

Having said that; Muslims already *believe* in Jesus. He's considered the holiest prophet of Islam, born of a virgin, and now alive in heaven, waiting to return for the day of judgment. More on that later. Let's get further into *Iman.*

17

1.   First, there is God. There is one true God, and there is none other. The Muslim believes that the *oneness* of God is of primary importance.   He is unique, he is whole within himself, lacking nothing. He has no equal, he has no division. Many Muslims believe that the Christian idea of the trinity "lessens" God, and that it is an offense against him to believe that he is divided in any way. This can partially be attributed to a misunderstanding. Muslims often believe that the Christian trinity is composed of God the Father, Jesus, and the virgin Mary. Muslims, however, do not equate any person to the stature of God – not Jesus, not Mary, not Muhammad. In fact, it is an offensive thing to brashly say anything about God which could be misconstrued to be irreverent, or that indicates that he shares his authority with anyone. Muslims believe that if you make a person a equal with God you have committed a terrible sin, known as *shirk,* or blasphemy against God. This one true God is all powerful, and all-knowing, with complete authority and ready to judge.

Christians, when they first encounter the differences between the Muslim and Christian perceptions of God, are often tempted to begin introducing the "Christian God."   I believe this is an unnecessary step – even a mistake. Why?

God is who he is.

There are various misunderstandings and lies *about* God, but none of them change the reality of who he is. By tearing down the concept of Allah (the Muslim's perception of God), we may endanger (or delay) the possibility that God can be revealed to our Muslim friends by the Holy Spirit, the same way Simon Peter discovered. "Flesh and blood cannot reveal this to you; it was by the Spirit."

Pressing the theological differences won't work. A recent study of Muslims who came to faith in Jesus Christ showed that the overwhelming majority came to Christ because of the Holy Spirit (personal revelation) and through miracles. A very minute number embraced Jesus due to the use of apologetics or doctrinal debate.

Once again, we see that faith in Jesus comes by seeing him, being touched by him, being led by the Spirit, and not through intellectual argument.

Doctrinal differences are secondary. The primary goal is to point people to Jesus, allowing him to do the work of the heart and mind.

2. The Angels. Angels are the servants of God . Through these servants, God reveals his will, most notably to the prophets. The greatest of the angels is the Archangel Gabriel, the one who revealed God to Muhammad, and who strengthened Jesus. Another great angel was Michael.

Within the same category, and yet of different kind, are the *jinn*, which, to quote the Qur'an: "And the jinn we created before, of intensely hot fire." (Q 15:27)

The jinn are notable in that they are not men, they are not angels, and they can be either good or evil because they are believed to have free will. Accordingly, jinn can be "saved" or condemned. There is a great fear of the jinn. . They are often connected with disasters and accidents and are believed to haunt abandoned places and deserts. Many Muslims will do whatever they can to avoid confronting the jinn, including many acts of superstition.

And, of course, there's the devil. In Arabic his name is *Iblis* or *Shaytan*. Traditionally, he is labeled as an angel or a jinn, and to the Muslim he is as evil as he is to Christians.

3. The Holy Books. This is one subject I cannot emphasize enough. Muslims treat their holy book with extreme reverence. It is common for Christians to set their Bibles on the carpet beneath their chairs , or to underline important passages of scripture. A Muslim would never do this with the Qur'an. The books are holy; they are representative of God, because they are his truths. When you are sharing the gospel with one of your Muslim friends, be sure to respect both the Bible and the Qur'an. Use a clean Bible, treat it with respect, and do not put it on the floor.

Originally, there were over one hundred books that were holy to Islam. Now, there are only a few left. They are:

The *Taureh*, which is what we would call the Torah, or the Pentateuch.

The *Zabur,* or the Psalms of David. David is considered prophetic to the Muslims, and his poems are considered holy.

The *Injil,* or the gospels. These are the teachings of Jesus of Nazareth which the Muslims revere as holy.

The *Hadith.* This is not simply a single book that is considered holy by all Muslims. Hadith are a series of traditions and precedents set in place by Muhammad's life. These traditions are many and varied, and there are varying levels of reverence for them. Some of these sayings and actions of the prophet are recorded (there are six 'official' Hadith) and all are called Hadith. Some are so serious that they are considered a valid basis for state law; even legislation and enforcement. Others, seem trite, or even silly. Make every attempt to approach the Hadith with an open and respectful mind: a misguided laugh or joke could setback your friendship.

The *Qur'an.* This is the holiest book in Islam. It is the final and complete revelation of God to men. According to the verse of abrogation (Q 13:39) all later verses supercede earlier ones. To Muslims, this includes earlier teachings besides only the Qur'an. In Islam, the Bible is subject to the Qur'an. In a case of disagreement, i.e. the Bible vs. The Qur'an, the Qur'an "wins".

Muslims will often say that Christians and Jews have distorted the original texts from God, and that is why the Qur'an is both necessary, as well as "more correct." However, the Qur'an itself does not say this. (See the following chapter for references.)

4. The prophets. The Muslim understanding of the prophets is that they are the men that God has used to influence history, as well as being mouthpieces for God's teaching. The prophets served as guides to keep men on the path of righteous living. The prophets have a prominent role in warning humans of the imminence of judgment, as well as the consequences of earning the wrath of God.

Of all of the prophets, there are six which are considered to be what we could call major prophets. These are: Adam, Noah, Abraham, Moses, Jesus, and Muhammad. Because Muhammad is the final prophet, he is regarded as the 'seal of the prophets,' the last one, who has rendered all prophecy complete and final.

Jesus (*Isa* in the Qur'an) is regarded as a holy prophet, without sin, born of a virgin, and interestingly enough, called the "word of God." (Q 4:171) And also a "word from God" (Q 3:55). In the same verse, it is emphasized that Jesus was an apostle, powerful, working miracles, but still only human. None of the prophets, while they are considered role-models for mankind, are divine.

What's astounding about the adherence to these prophets is that Muslims are not permitted to deny any of them. Read down the list again, and see how many of those prophets you can read for yourself in your nearest Bible. The best tools are probably already within your reach.

5. The day of judgment. This is the greatly feared day in which God will weigh every man's deeds and determine his eternal fate. In the Qur'an, it is linked to the resurrection, and there will be warnings, very similar to the revelations of John on the Isle of Patmos. There will be natural disasters and wars, and even an appearance of the antichrist. Following this, the resurrected ones will walk the earth for forty years, while the recordings of their deeds will be weighed. Every person will then cross a narrow bridge. Good Muslims will be saved instantly, and some will fall into hell for a short period of time. All infidels (people who don't believe in God – usually not in reference to Christians or Jews) will fall into hell and stay there for eternity.

6. Predestination (Taqdir) Because God is supreme and all-powerful, fate is understood to be predetermined by God, and therefore, God's will is final and absolute. Because of the predominance of this article of faith, the philosophy of fatalism has become widespread and pervasive. *Maqdur;* or as we would say in English, "It's been decided." For a Muslim, the concept of freely choosing your own fate seems to fly in the face of God's supremacy, and so the common belief is that things have been ordained for every creature.

A Christ-like perspective

Be sensitive
Because we believe, as do Muslims, that there is only one God, we have an opportunity to enjoy much shared ground. Notice I said *enjoy*. I did not say *exploit*. It is very critical that you keep in mind how sacred the faith of the Muslim is to him. Do not treat it with disregard.

Having said that, the best piece of advice I can give you is to think before you speak. Because God is holy, and because he is One (at unity with himself) you should stay on that topic. Don't open a can of worms by using a polemic explanation, i.e., beginning by explaining the concept of the Trinity. There will be time enough for such discussions down the road, but at the beginning of a relationship stick with things about the scriptures, God and Jesus. Tread lightly around the issues of the cross, the deity and the sonship of Christ. I'm not encouraging you to be wishy-washy about your faith, rather, be sensitive to the Holy Spirit and go at His pace.

The method that I find to be the most effective, and even the most Christ-like, is to stay on target with Jesus. I talk about him, about his leadership style, his wisdom, his teachings and his miracles. When I do this, I always do my best to *include* others in my ideals and words. I have sat and prayed with many influential Muslim businessmen and political leaders, and never once have I been chastised for talking about Isa al-Mesiah: Jesus the Christ.

When Jesus becomes an object of centrality in anyone, a polarizing effect takes place: the people with whom you are involved will either be uncomfortable, or they will be interested. I'm not saying that their current attitude about Jesus is a litmus test of their faith; I believe that Jesus brings all things necessary with himself. And that's why I take *only him* into the relationship.

Muslims are often more interested in angels than we are. It's not often that any sore subject comes to the surface over angels, but in case it does – once again, be sensitive. You may just want to take it back to the core issue, rather than focusing on the disparities of the two faiths.

Feel free to discuss the prophets. Muslims enjoy discussing the qualities of the prophets, and there is plenty of room to talk about Moses, Abraham, Jesus, David, and Muhammad. However, I must warn you – don't be irreverent, and if one of your friends challenges you on a point of dispute:

don't be defensive. In fact, I've tried to make it a personal goal to *never* argue with my Muslim friends. Whatever their objections may be, I try to nudge the discussion back to the person, works and words of Jesus of Nazareth.

Know the Qur'an. At least read some of it. If you don't have a copy, get one. Don't worry if you can't read Arabic, just pick up an English copy, and read some of the text. By meeting someone halfway in a discussion about *their* holy book, you will find more freedom in your relationship, as well as some gratitude for being open with them. Although the more fundamental reaches of Islam hold that only the Arabic Qur'an is correct (this is actually Islamic doctrine, that the Qur'an exists in the heavens in Arabic), you will gain miles of respect by showing your sincerity. Despite the Arabic propensity for emotionalism, you will find that a sincere Muslim enjoys a sincere conversation.

Avoid the stereotypical distinctions. I learned a long time ago that thinking of myself as a "Christian missionary" was the quickest way to lose the interest of new friends, let alone an audience.

For centuries, in many minds on both sides of the planet, it's been a conflict of Christianity vs. Islam, and using the wrong terminology, or making distinctions about who did what, and why who's right and who's not and all of that other stuff will just put you in a bind. Guaranteed. And it will make you defensive, at which time you lose your point.

I simply tell people that I'm a follower of Jesus, and usually, with a little explanation, things aren't so guarded and tense. Jesus doesn't come loaded with bias, prejudice, conflict, or war. Christianity often does.

The five pillars

The very structure of Islam is based upon five pillars of religion, five basic tenets which Muslims are required to observe. For a handful of small fundamentalist sects, there is a sixth pillar, which is *jihad,* or holy war. We'll address this in detail later.

These five pillars are inherently expressed within the Qur'an itself, and you will find that those who are devoted to these five pillars are exemplary people, and may not feel or even appear as though they are in need of more or different religion. This is, in fact, true. Jesus is what they need, the same as you and me.

The pillars of faith could be best compared to the tenets of Judaism or the Christian doctrines: They're not the same in substance, but they follow the same form as the other classical religions: they are guidelines for faith, and in Islamic States, they are law, which is either obeyed, or enforced. Those who live outside of these tenets, if they are allowed to maintain their own faith, are typically required to pay *zakat* in the form of taxation.

The pillars are regarded in the majority of the Muslim world to be necessary. They are similar in many ways to Jewish Law in that they are mandated and to disregard them is to sin against God.

Islam is a solidly works-based religion. As in most religions, there is not always a passion for genuine spirituality, but rather a fear of God's wrath and the consequences that follow. I am often aware of a very heavy sense of works-related "religiosity." In mosques, there are scales on the walls (representing how God will judge each person in the end by his deeds), prayer mats on the floor, and every space is pervaded with a sense of devotion that seems to be born of equal parts anxiety and desire.

But we have a key: **grace.** Like Muslims, we have prophets of law, and that law can guide us to the grace and truth of Jesus Christ.

In the western court of opinion, the concept of Islam typically conveys images of mujahedin in black robes with AK-47's and scimitars sweeping through the desert on a nomadic raid, killing babies and pillaging tents. We have this idea in the west that Muslims are loose-cannon radicals with destruction in mind and automatic weapons in hand.

While it's true that there are a few terrorists who utilize the banner of Islam to kill and destroy, the fact of the matter is, that the majority of Muslims are far more concerned with obeying the commandments of God, and many are so close to the truths of Jesus that it's within reach of their hearts.

If we were to compare religions side by side in terms of actual behavior, you would see that many Muslims are actually more religious (in terms of religious practices, i.e. prayers, traditions and duties) than many Christians. This devotion is typical for Arabs, and is a part of the Arab temperament. It is Islam – submission to God.

In fact, let's take it one step further, just to make sure we're on the same page. As westerners, we often use blanket statements, "those Muslims…" or, "Why can't Islam stop the fighting …" and so on and so forth. The problem is that such statements equate the sins of the individual to the fault of the whole, when such is simply not the case. There is a key distinction between the vast majority of Muslims, (who want peace and prosperity, like you and I), and the extremists, (who believe that all people, including other Muslims, are condemned).

I have many friends who are Catholic, and if, during the seventies and eighties, you were to blame Catholicism for the terrorism in Belfast, you would have been completely wrong. Everybody knows, Catholics are not terrorists. So, while we're at it, Muslims are not terrorists. Terrorists are terrorists.

Having said that, let me get back to my point: - the five pillars of Islam.

1. The Testimony (*Shahadah*). *There is no god but God, and Muhammad is the prophet of God.* This is a confession of belief in God. This is the basic and first step of Islam, to say with your mouth and believe in your heart that there is only one true God, and that Muhammad is his final messenger. To many Muslims, this alone makes you a Muslim. Obviously, we can agree with the first, but not the second part of this statement. There *is* no god but God. Allegiance to a specific prophet, however, or even prophets in general, is not a requirement according to a biblical relationship with God. I have, on many occasions, been welcomed into a Muslim home because I simply agreed with the first part of this statement. There is no God but God.

2. The Fast (*Sawm*, observed primarily through *Ramadan*) According to tradition, Ramadan is the commemorative fast of the revelations given from God through Gabriel to Muhammad. Muslims are required to observe a dusk-till-dawn fast from food, drink, tobacco, and other items. After sunset, meals are permitted, and prayer is invoked for forgiveness of sins already committed and sins not yet committed.

In some of the nations under the rule of Islamic Law (*Sharia*) there are very strict enforcements regulated for those who trespass the fast of Ramadan, and the consequences can be costly.

3. Almsgiving (*Zakat*). This varies in each country, and also by class and income, but by and large, each Muslim is required to give at least 2.5% of their assets to the poor. The poor could be defined as the sick, travelers, or new converts to Islam. During my years in the Middle East, I have been befriended by numerous Muslims, some of whom were people of means. What I noticed right away about these people was their propensity to give upon request. One of my friends, a wealthy businessman, employs a supervisor to oversee his *voluntary* almsgivings; meaning that my friend does not only give his required percentage, but he donates, based upon need, out of compassion.

Despite the fact that almsgiving is obligatory, there are many Muslims who give out of compassion. In fact, this is one of the greatest paths of friendship you can have with a Muslim. I used to meet regularly with political and business leaders in Lebanon, (even leaders in the Hamas and Hezballah), in order to pray for the refugees and the poor. The center of every discussion was compassion; how we could ease suffering, open schools, and provide medical attention. This is key: Jesus is exemplified by compassion, even legendary for it. He can be a critical discussion point when you are conversing with a devout Muslim about suffering and compassion.

Muslims are typically people of honor, and a portion of that honor is found in the readiness of compassion. This, in my estimation, is often above the 2.5% standard set by the commandments.

4. Prayer (*Salat*)

As most people know, Muslims are required to pray five times a day: at sunrise, shortly after noon, mid-afternoon, after sundown, and after nightfall. (Although Shi'ites are more likely to pray only three times in a day). Only the most serious Muslims actually stop and pray five times a day. As is the case with many people in any religion, prayer often becomes a mere ritual and is sometimes relegated to the holy day, which, in Islam, is Friday.

Unlike the prayers we're used to in the west; the daily prayers of Islam are conveyed in ritual format. First, the call to prayer is chanted from the minaret of the mosque. Depending on the mosque, sometimes there is amplification so that the people in the outlying areas can be prepared for prayer as well. The nearby Muslims respond to the *azan*, (the call) and the prayer commences, a series of statements and responses.

Muslims face towards Mecca when they pray. Every mosque has a marker designating the proper direction, and most Muslims constantly know which direction is the correct direction – even if they're indoors.

Tradition holds that Muslims have always prayed in the direction of Mecca because it is the birthplace of the prophet. However, most researchers and historians now agree that for a short time, in the beginning, they prayed in the direction of Jerusalem – the city of David and Jesus. However, due to some conflict with the Jews in Medina, the original followers decided to pray toward the city of Muhammad's birth – a little more southeast.

The posture of the prayer is important to all sects and varieties of Muslims. The forehead must contact the ground, and some Muslims wear a long robe so that they can remove their pants and shoes. All Muslims remove their shoes in order to respect what is holy during prayer.

The prayers are recitations, and they are pronounced in sets and intervals. Each individual responds in confession of God's greatness, wisdom, and a plea for mercy. The steps are followed with a prostrated bow, acknowledging God's greatness.

If ever you have an opportunity to observe Muslim prayers – take the chance. If you are polite, respectful, and courteous you may gain a friend, and you may well find yourself in the privileged position to learn a few things – both for your relationship with your Muslim friend, as well as your relationship with God.

5. Pilgrimage (*Hajj*). All Muslims who are able are required to make a journey to Mecca. The capability of travel, by tradition, has been the means to afford the journey, as well as the physical ability to travel. Some allow a pilgrimage by proxy, and there are concessions for those who are ill or otherwise unable to make the trip.

Only Muslims can go into "the house" or "Kaba". No outsider has had any claim to having seen the black stone which "fell from heaven." Muslims are encouraged to kiss this black stone, which, according to tradition, was once white but has been turned black by the touch of sinful men. If the crowd is too thick, they must touch it with a hand or a walking stick.

After visiting the Kaba, there are several other visits, which most Muslims make, including Mt. Arafat, and Mina, to throw stones at a series of three pillars, one of which is thought to represent the devil. Finally, there is a visitation to the tomb of Muhammad at Medina. Saudi Arabia reports that over two million people participate in the annual pilgrimage.

Again, like all religions, Islam has developed many traditions or "byproducts." These have come about as a result of 1400 years of practicing Islam. Often , these byproducts are what the western world perceives to be Islam itself.

The foremost is the concept of *jihad*. The word literally means "struggle" in Arabic, and it was conceptually, in origin, the idea of religious struggle, much like the early church after the ascension of Christ. However, there is no doubt that the primary meaning associated with jihad today is: holy war. The headlines and casualties of terrorism are the first things we think of when we heard the word. This is, without a doubt, a byproduct of the military campaigns of Muhammad, and in recent times, with the global struggle of some Muslims to resurrect the historical power of Islam to create an international community with a legitimate and recognized caliphate. I must say at this point, that of the thousands of Muslims I've known over the years and in the many Muslim counties I've traveled in – I've seldom (if ever) met a Muslim who believes that Islam should conquer the world by the sword.

Some places in the Islamic world today maintain a definite anti-modern approach to life, and this could be associated with Muhammad's original intent to return his countrymen back to the old ways and the one true God. In fact there is a sense among these nations that the western "modern" world has fallen off the track due to materialism and science. Some see our immoral television programming and associate it with our "modern ways." Additionally, the culture at the time of Islam's inception was tribal. Leadership was based on eldership. Nation-states were ruled by a monarchy, typically a familial monarchy with royalty, and a very definite social strata of castes. Today this can be seen in the tendency of Islamic states to rule by direct dictatorship. Even Iraq, which has until late, been secular under the rule of Saddam Hussein, was a dictatorship governing (or suppressing) various factions and sects, Primarily the Kurdish north and the Shiite south.

Due to the strong tribal aspects of most Muslim countries and the Muslims' high view of authority and sovereignty, democracy is often a difficult proposition. Iraq is an obvious case in point. The entire concept of representative government does not gel with strong religious leadership, much of which comes directly from the Muslim concept of God. God is not elected, he simply *is,* and his authority is unquestionable. The ideology of individualism, which we so value in the West, and which leads more naturally into a democratic society, is virtually non-existent in the Islamic world.

Many of my western friends are shocked when they first encounter the Muslim concept of *Maqtub* – or what we could arguably call fatalism.

My Muslim friends have explained to me that it means simply, "as God wills it," or "such is my lot," or even, "it has been decided upon."

For the Muslim, God has a clearly predetermined will, and he acts upon it without question. Therefore, the Muslim does not question it either, even if it does not make sense.

One of my good friends, an American Air Force pilot, once told me that he'd flown on training sorties with his pilot equivalents in Saudi Arabia. At one time, while flying with a Saudi pilot, during an equipment malfunction, the jet appeared to be on a direct collision course with the terrain. While my friend busied himself with emergency procedures, he noticed that his Saudi counterpart was seated calmly with his hands in his lap, putting no effort into changing their course.

"What are you doing?" my friend shouted, "we're going to crash!"

"If so," replied the Saudi pilot, "it is as Allah wills."

Although Muslims believe in prayer, there really isn't a theology in which the "fervent prayer of a righteous man," has any avail on God's will. It has been decided, there is no changing it. Allah is resolute, and his will is unquestionable.

A Christ-like perspective

Pillars are for building

First of all: know these five pillars. If you sincerely want to develop friendships with Muslims, then you need areas of common interest, and it would behoove you to know what it is that they believe and are commanded to do.

Don't attempt to argue with the testimony. In truth, the testimony is correct, in that there *is* only one God, and his name, in Arabic, *is* Allah. As far as Muhammad goes, be careful. If you're the type that wants to confront Muhammad because you believe he *wasn't* a prophet, then you should change the subject, because to most Muslims it's not up for debate. It will take a revelation from the Holy Spirit before this is up for discussion.

Muhammad said many things which *were* true, particularly some of his teachings about Jesus. Whether God holds him as a prophet or not won't be a productive discussion point – particularly early on in a relationship, because his followers believe that he was, and it doesn't hurt my testimony to allow that. It's not up to me to disprove their beliefs, but to show them the Father through Christ which comes by a revelation of the Spirit of God and my clear testimony.

Muhammad taught that Jesus was born of a virgin, (Q 19:20) worked miracles (Q 3:49; 5:110), had no sin (Q 19:19), was the Word of God (Q 4:171), and even went so far as to call him "Jesus the Messiah" (Q 3:45).

Since the above things are in fact *true*, there's no point in us fooling around with who gets recognized for what. That's God's job.

Regarding the fast, there is some basic etiquette which you should remember: don't eat in front of any of your Muslim friends during Ramadan, or any other voluntary fasts.

Be careful not to walk in front of a praying Muslim. Go around, or wait.

When praying yourself, stand, kneel, or hold out your hands with the palms upwards. Let your Muslim friends know that you pray (without being a hypocrite). Muslims often think that Christians don't ever pray, because we don't do it publicly in the same way.

Respect the almsgiving. In fact, participate when you can. As always, you should be quick to regard what is virtuous and you should not take it upon yourself to point out what is not. Humbly share with them the times you give tithes and offerings, while sharing your motivation for doing so.

Lastly, realize that for every Muslim practice, there is something Jesus has said something which is relevant. Because the teachings of Jesus are important to your Muslim friends, you have all the conversation material you need. Specifically, read with them what Jesus says about giving to the poor, praying, fasting, and acknowledging God.

III. THE HOLY BOOK

THE WORDS OF GOD

Tainted history

Of all of the elements of Islam, I can think of none more in need of discussion than the Muslim holy book, the Qur'an. Over the centuries, we in the west have been influenced by historical accounts, incorrect doctrine, and the mass media to believe the wrong sort of things about Islam. This has not been helped by recent wars and terrorism, either.

However, once we have the scales of prejudice removed from our eyes, it becomes easier to take an honest look at what is taught in the Qur'an, what our Muslim friends believe, and how we can interface with them as friends and followers of Jesus.

This is difficult at first. For the westerner, there is a tremendous amount of bias and prejudice based on centuries of tainted history and two-sided conflict. In our case, the western disposition against Islam is as old as the crusades. The various churches, in various traditions, have held that the Muslim is a killer, a raider, a hater, a radical zealot, and a terrorist. Add to that the fact that there are some Islamic radicals who actually fit that description on the evening news, and you have a very strong resentment of the Muslim world emanating from the misinformed perspective of the west.

In his excellent work *Building Bridges,* the late pastor Fouad Elias Accad, of Lebanon, wrote a fitting example of this traditional bias.

Suppose a man who had shaved off all his hair and who wrapped himself in a bright orange sarong came into my community proclaiming "God's Truth." No matter how sincere and loving he was, I would be dead set against renouncing my culture to accept his "truth" about God and becoming like him. But, if he had behaved according to the ways of my culture, and treated my beliefs with respect, it would be far easier to hear what he was saying and to seriously consider it.[i]

In the western mindset, the shaved head and the orange robe immediately label the individual as, "a pagan, Buddhist or new age monk," and leave little room for us to take that person seriously – if we even listen at all. The same goes for Muslims – traditional or otherwise. We hear the accent, we see the clothing, the behavior, and all of the alarms go off.

It is with the same colored lenses that we look at the holiest book of Islam, the Qur'an. Regarded in the west as everything from blasphemy to hate speech, there are very few people who are knowledgeable about the true nature of the Qur'an.

In reality, the Qur'an can be very helpful. Though few Christians know this, quite possibly the greatest inroad we have to reach the heart of our Muslim friends is this book. Having said that, I have to qualify it: there are many things in the Qur'an which are confusing, and even contradictory. There are verses which condone murder, and there are verses which deny the things we know to be true, for instance, a statement that it was Ishmael and not Isaac who was taken up the mountain with Abraham for a sacrifice. The Qur'an also disputes the crucifixion, citing that God tricked the Jews. Despite these theological differences, there is a gold mine running through the Qur'an: his name is Jesus (Isa). The Qur'an mentions Jesus some 83 times – depending on how you count – and all of them with great reverence.

Muhammad was not, (at least not early in his career), building a religion in order to displace Judaism and Christianity. The vast majority of his teachings were along the same lines as the two other monotheistic religions. In fact, Muhammad viewed his teachings to be "more of the same," simply directed to his Arab countrymen. As far as we know, for six hundred years after the time of Christ, there were no testaments, teachings, holy books, prophecies or gospels in *Arabic*. We know for a fact that Muhammad viewed himself as having an obligation to turn his countrymen away from their idolatry back to the ways of, "the people of the book" which is what the Qur'an labels Christians and Jews.

We cannot say exactly when or why Muhammad began to differ from the beliefs of the others, but we do know, that by the time the Qur'an was compiled (650 or so) there were some key differences which have now been castigated as being the entirety of Islam. For instance, many Qur'anic verses make statements which, if they were to be called "cornerstone doctrine" would make for a very different religion of Islam. This would be like saying that the only thing that Christians believe in is hell.

We must begin by asking Jesus to give us his viewpoint. The Holy Spirit will give us, if we ask him, a way to love Muslims without these prejudices. Prejudice will find a way to taint and disease our relationships with our Muslim friends, and they could even distort what it is that we're saying about Jesus. Obviously, we don't have to convert to Islam in order to reach Muslims, but being conscientious about the history of conflict between Islam and Christianity, and doing our best to stay open-minded and without preconception will give us a lot more mileage than merely jumping in with an argumentative or apologetic approach disputing the Qur'an.

There are some things which Muslims often believe to be true about the Qur'an, and which are in reality, not so. Many

Muslims, while they view our Bible as a holy book, are reticent about it because they believe that it has been changed. They believe that either we or the Jews have changed it, and by comparison, they point to the Qur'an, which they believe to be the perfect and unimpeachable recording of God's words.

History shows us with empirical evidence that this is not so. During the last twenty years of his life, Muhammad was given these messages in installments. According to the Muslim belief, the Qur'an exists eternally in heaven in the form of stone tablets. It is written in Arabic in heaven as well. Muhammad passed on these revelations literally by word of mouth. Muslim tradition maintains that the angel Gabriel helped him to collect and record these revelations, word for word, exactly as the stone tablets in heaven read.

According to history, however, it is known that there was no complete Qur'an written at the time of Muhammad's death. As time went on, different individuals wrote the teachings of Muhammad, and there was some variation between scripts. Perhaps not significant variances, but it wasn't until 650 or so that there was an "official" version which rendered all others obsolete.

Fragments of these early Qur'anic scripts have been found, dating back to the eighth century. The script in which these fragments were written excluded punctuation and vowels, interestingly enough, and according to some, this makes for a transcription which could be translated a number of ways.

There are 114 *surahs* in the Qur'an. These are chapters of varying length, and they all have titles, for instance, *Yusuf* is the twelfth surah – the story of Joseph. Some surahs are lengthy, some are very short – a few verses in all. They are arranged in order of length, with the longer surahs in the beginning and the shorter ones at the end. Some of them are poetic, like the Psalms. Others deal more with the concrete issues of life and the practical aspects of religion.

The verses themselves are called *ayas*, or *ayat*. The Arabic word *aya* is best translated as "sign."

One thing you ought to be careful to observe is that Muslims do not associate the Qur'an and it's writings with any human authors, as we do with the various books of the Bible. (The book of Job; Peter, Jude, James, etcetera). Muslim tradition holds that the Qur'an comes directly from God, that the words are from God – that he is the one speaking. It is blasphemous to attribute the Qur'an even to Muhammad.

For the purposes of time and space, this chapter will contain some bullet points and references of suggested reading about the life of Jesus, but I encourage you to pick up a copy of the Qur'an and do some homework yourself.

I've prepared a list of verses in both the Qur'an as well as correlating verses in the New Testament, and I've broken them down by topic. For reference, the first number is the number of the Surah, (like a chapter) and the second is the verse. So, *Q 3:53* means *Surah III, ayat 53*.

Birth:
God foreordained (Isa) Jesus' birth 3:47; 714; Matt 1:23
God commanded Jesus' birth 3:47; Luke 1:31, 35
Jesus' birth was a miracle to mankind 21:91; Luke 2:8-20; Matt 2:1-12
The day of Jesus' birth was blessed 19:33; Luke 2:10-14
Jesus is the son of Mary, (Mariam) 3:36; 3:45; Luke 2:7; Matt 13:55
Jesus confirms his own legitimacy (in the cradle) 19:29; Matt 1:18-25

Character:
God made Jesus an example to the people of Israel 43:49
God commanded Jesus to honor his mother 19:32; John 19:26

God did not make Jesus proud nor rebellious 19:32; Mark 7:36
Jesus is righteous 3:46; 6:85; John 8:46
Jesus only did what God told him to do 5:117; John 14:1,10

Conception:
No man had touched Mary (Mariam) when she became pregnant with Jesus 19:20; 21:91
God sent His spirit to Mary and It took the form of a man 19:27; Luke 1:26-35
God sent his spirit to give Mary a sinless son 19:19; 66:12; Luke 1:35
Jesus was sent down from heaven 3:53
God created Jesus, 3:47, but also see 21:91; Matthew 1:18

Death:
People plotted against Jesus 3:54; John 12:10
God would have been able to destroy/kill Jesus 5:17, Luke 1:37
God said to Jesus that he would make him die 3:55; Mark 14:36
When God made Christ die, God himself became the overseer 5:117; John 17:14
*(Jesus was) one of the messengers who was killed by Israel 2:87; 5:70; Acts 7:52; Luke 11:49
*The Jews killed (Jesus) among other prophets 2:91; Acts 3:15; 2:36; 4:10; 5:30
*The Jews themselves *did not* kill or crucify Christ 4:157; Luke 23:24-25
*Their (and Christ's) killers weren't the actual killers because *God* killed them 8:17, but also see 4:157, 158; Acts 2:23
*(Christ) was dead and God raised him 6:122; Romans 6:4-11
The day Jesus died was blessed 19:33; Luke 2:10-14

Exalted:

Jesus is the knowledge of the last day 43:61; Luke 21:25-28, 17:30

The knowledge of the last days is God's 41:47 (See above also) Matt 24:36

God aided Jesus with the Holy Spirit 2:87, 253; 5:110; 1Peter 1:2; Matt 4:1, 12:18; Luke 4:18

John the Baptist (Yahya) testified of Jesus 3:39; John 1:29-34

God preferred Jesus above the other messengers 2:253; Heb 1:1,2,3: Matt 21:33-41

Jesus pronounces peace upon himself 19:33; John 13:13-17

*Jesus intercedes with God according to God's will 2:255; 1 Tim 2:5; Heb 7:25; Romans 8:27,34

God exalted Jesus 2:253; Phil 2:9

Jesus is distinguished in the world 3:45; John 5:22

Jesus is near to God (see above) John 14:7-9

Jesus is blessed 43:61 also with 43:85; Matt 21:9

God made Jesus blessed wherever he went 19:31; Mark 7:37

God made a covenant with them (incl. Jesus) 33:7; Luke 4:18,43

Followers:

God's helpers are those who help Jesus 3:52; 61:14; 1John 2:23

Jesus had followers 3:53; John 3:26

God said to Jesus that he would make his followers higher than the unbelievers until judgment day 3:55; Eph 2:6

Jesus told God that the disciples were God's servants and he could choose to torture or forgive them 5:118; John 17:6-11

The Christians say that Jesus (Messiah) is the son of God (Allah) 9:30; Gal 4:47

The Christians took Jesus the son of Mary as Lord instead of God 9:31; 1 Cor 8:6

Fulfillment:

Jesus confirmed the old testament that was in his hands 3:50; 5:46; Luke 4:21, 16:17; Matt 15:1-6; 5:18

Humanity:

Jesus ate food 5:75; Luke 24:43

Jesus spoke to the people when an adult 3:46; 5:110; Matt 5-7; John 14:10

God gave Jesus refuge 23:50: Luke 4:30

God is Jesus' Lord 5:117; Phil 1:3

God gave commandments to Jesus 42:13; Heb 1:5,8,12,13

God commanded Jesus to pray and give alms while he remained alive 19:31; John 17:1-6, 13:29: Luke 6:12; Matt 19:21

Judgment day:

On judgment day, Jesus will witness against those who did not believe in him before their death 4:159; John 5:22,23

Miracles:

Jesus created a clay bird for the Jews, and breathed life into it 3:49; 5110; John 5:21, 20:22

Jesus gave sight to a man born blind (see above reference) John 9:1-12

Jesus healed a leper, raised the dead, and prophesied (see above 3:49; 5:110) John 11:43-44; John 6:47-49; Mark 12:40

Christ asked God to provide a meal from heaven 5:112-114; John 6:5-14

God gave miracles to Jesus 2:87,253; John 6:11-14

Jesus came with miracles 43:63; 61:16; Matt 12:22-32

Names:

Christ is Jesus' title 4:157,171; John 4:25

His name is *Messiah,* Jesus, son of Mary 3:45; Matt 1:21

Jesus is a spirit from God 4:171; Luke 1:35

A mercy from God 19:21; Acts 2:23

Jesus was a miracle to all men 21:91; Luke 2:8-20

Christ was a witness over the people while with them 5:117; John 17:12,13

Prophet:

God aided Jesus with the Holy Spirit 2:87,253; 5:110; 1Peter 1:2; Matt 4:1,12; Luke 4:18

God caused Jesus to follow in the lineage of Jewish prophets 5:46; Matt 21:33-41

Jesus was a prophet 2:91; Luke 11:49

Jesus told the people of Israel that a prophet was coming to them whose name was praised 61:6; John 14:16;17

Relationship to God:

God is *not* Christ the son of Mary 5:17,72; 1Cor 8:6

Jesus is a spirit from God 4:171; Luke 1:35

God asked Jesus if he had told people to take himself and Mary as two Gods in place of God 5:116; John 10:30; 17:21; Matt 17:5

Jesus answered that he never said anything he had nor right to say 5:116; John 14:10

God commanded Jesus to honor his mother 19:32; John 19:26

Resurrection:

God raised Jesus to himself 4:158; Mark 16:19

God plotted against the people's plot, and won 3:54; Rev 13:8; Matt 20:17-19; Acts 3:15, 4:10; Romans 8:37

The day that Jesus was raised was blessed 19:33; Luke 2:10-14

God said to Jesus that he would raise him up alive 3:55; Acts 1:9; Luke 18:33

Revelation:

God gave Jesus the Bible 19:30; Matt 5:21-48

God revealed to the disciples of Jesus to believe in God and in his messenger, Jesus 5:111; John 6:68-69

God gave Jesus the new testament, in which is guidance and light 5:46; Luke 2:32

God taught Jesus the Bible and wisdom 3:48; 5:110

Jesus allowed a *(teaching and wisdom? from the Taureh) forbidden thing to them 3:50; Mark 7:14-20

Christ said that he brought the people wisdom 43:63; Matt 13:1-52

Servanthood:

Jesus said that he was God's servant 19:30; John 20:17; Phil 2:5-7

Jesus was not too arrogant to be God's servant 4:172; Phil 2:6-7

Jesus is only a servant to those God gave grace 43:59 (see also 4:171); Phil 2:5-11

Sinless:

Christ was sinless 19:19; Heb 7:26; 2Cor 5:21; John 8:46

The Word:

Jesus is a saying of the truth 19:34; 1John 5:7-12,20, 2:21, 1:1; 2John 1 Jesus is a word from God 3:39,45; John 1:14

Jesus is God's word 4:171; John 1:1-3

God spoke/cast his word to Mary 4:171; Luke 1:35; John 1:14

Although there are many more interesting items within the Qur'an, specifically about the Qur'an itself, God's nature, Christians and Jews (people of the Book), and heaven and hell, I believe that by far the most important item for us to center our attention on is Jesus (Isa) himself. After all, he is the Gospel.

A Christ-like perspective

The cultural barrier

Of critical importance to the follower of Jesus who wishes to befriend a Muslim is the knowledge of the religious, political, and cultural barriers. It is not merely a different society, a different clique of individuals, but it is so vastly a different culture, that you may well feel as though you are trying to speak to a person from another planet. That is the way the world is – the east and west have always been different, and God willing, they always will be, to some degree.

The first step is to make it a personal journey with Jesus at the helm. By being sensitive, using your instincts within the relationship, and by trusting the guidance of the Holy Spirit, you have all the things necessary to build a friendship.

Although I repeatedly use the term "friendship" I am not in any sense intending the connotations of the so-called "friendship evangelism" method, which I believe to be a mistaken method of bringing people into the kingdom using a relationship as a collateral to motivate conversion.

I'm talking about a real *friendship*.

Unlike the western world, where you can go to a church for fifteen years and still only know two people; where your individual credentials make you a desirable person or not, the eastern world has had a far longer stretch of time to think about the nature of relationships: family and friends.

In the Middle East, the prevailing tribal system has endured for thousands of years – literally. By far the most important credential one can possess is their lineage. In other words: your last name says more than your resume'.

Having said that, there is a recent influx of western perspective and corporate style business which has, in some ways, stirred the pot.

The family values of the Arab cultures are common across the region, and these values come with consequences.

Honor and courage are among the chief virtues of any Arab. Conversely, shame is an issue which cuts deep into the heart, and even the historical failures of the Arab people bring a sharp stab of pain if flippantly addressed.

All cultures look to heaven and, in one sense or another, see parts of their own image while looking for God. There's a reason that each culture has its own characterization of God, and ours is no different.

In the Islamic personification of God, he is vast and unknowable. His wrath is emphasized rather than his love, although he is, in the Qur'an, attributed with mercy and forgiveness. God's completeness and unity within himself render him so far untouchable and even aloof that the very idea of God coming to earth in human form is unthinkable. I know it is difficult to hear this, and even more difficult to find it palatable enough to put into practice, but, if you intend to carry on conversations with a Muslim, you should avoid phrases like "son of God," or others that refer to the Triune aspect of God, or "shared" godhood. I'm not suggesting that you *deny* what you know to be true about God, but rather to be sensitive to the differences in the two faiths, particularly at the beginning of a friendship. We want to go at the pace of the Holy Spirit – not ahead of him. We should remember the times in our lives when we, too, could only handle bits and pieces of this new truth of Jesus.

Actually, at this point, I like to take a different route than most Christians. The popular method is to try to explain what the Christian beliefs are, and to argue the veracity and superiority of the Christian faith. This is what E. Stanley Jones, in *The Christ of the Indian Road,* noted as a method which demolishes the beliefs of the other, and then attempts to build a structure on the smoldering wreckage.

Don't do this. I recommend that you *don't* try to argue that Jesus actually *is* the son of God. Don't deny it either, but remember that God will reveal himself to each individual in a unique way; and that we are only participating. God will save some pieces of information for later, allowing each person to digest the truth one piece at a time.

I believe that the most important question of all history is found in the annals of the New Testament, and was aimed at Peter.

Jesus asked, "Who do you say that I am?"

I believe that if we can introduce people to Jesus, he will take the responsibility of asking each person the same question. Jesus revealed himself to every person who earnestly sought him – should we believe now that he has ceased to do so?

With that in mind, I make it my responsibility only to point people to Jesus, allowing him to reveal himself through his teachings, his miracles, and his Spirit.

My point is that if you earnestly wish to open some communication with your Muslim friends, you are going to have to be sacrificial about it. Some of the most important phrases in your faith are going to have to be put on the shelf for a while. As Paul did, you have to be willing to be all things to all people in order that you might gain some. To the earnest Muslim, however, this cannot be a mere act on your part. In my experience, everybody has a "fake-o-meter" and can tell when you're putting on an act for them.

Throughout my time in the Middle East, whenever we would host interns or different youth teams at our facility, I always had one rule:

Be honest, be real. Confess *your* faults. Downplay *your* religion, and respect your friends' religion. Always assume that the person you are speaking with has a more "holy" life than you do, and treat them like it. Be the low man on the totem pole. Be the servant.

I was always surprised at the fruit that appeared from this approach. Once our Muslim friends realized we were actually interested in them, and that we were genuine, they were much more willing to pray together and study the life of Jesus.

I can only assume that some people will read this and will believe that my approach may be wrong or doctrinally incorrect. However, please take these thoughts of mine and pray about them. If you disagree with anything I say, your best bet is to compare these things side by side with the teachings of Jesus, and always go with what you're getting from him.

IV. WOMEN OF THE FAITH

WOMEN AND ISLAM

A different kind of life

One of the most popular questions I receive is: "what's Islam like for women?"

Although everyone shares the same concern, there are those who ask the question not only out of concern for the women in question, but also out of criticism of Islam. This is understandable, to say the least; one of Islam's glaring flaws *is* its medieval perspective on women's rights. But this is not universal, and I am happy to say that there are many Arab/Muslim nations which have become aware of this deficiency, and are moving to correct it.

As for the question on the whole, there's really no simple one-word answer. There are different kinds of Islamic nations. Some are more liberal, like Tunisia, Lebanon or Jordan. Some are more fundamentalist: Saudi Arabia, Iran and Sudan. Some are completely secular, for instance, Albania.

Within the community of Islamic nations, there are those which structure their government and justice according to *Sharia*, Islamic Law.

Sharia is derived not only from the teachings of the Qur'an, but also from the *Hadith,* the traditions of Muhammad himself. *Sharia* was constructed during a period of time in which Islam was on the rise and mobile, both politically and militarily. It not only details the regulations required of each

Muslim for personal devotion, but also the theological curricula for governance.

Nations who follow the blueprints of *Sharia* have a parochial perspective on such western ideals as women's rights. This is because the model for Islamic Law is about twelve centuries old. Sadly, Islamic law was not codified during Islam's golden era, when science, learning and tolerance were values of the Islamic empire. Rather, Islamic law was constructed during a time when women were not equal to men, an era when men could have numerous wives and could beat or divorce them.

There are some facts that you should know about women in Islam, particularly if you plan on being a friend.

For the most part, the woman's place is the home. This is enforced in some countries – the late Taliban in particular forced women out of their jobs, out of their schools and back into their homes, where they were required to stay except with a male escort from the family.

In most Muslim nations, it is not *required* for women to stay home, but it is often the reality. Throughout my years in the Middle East, I noticed how different groups of Muslims varied in their traditions. Most of our friends were the more liberal or even nominal variety, and the manners of the women were typically western-leaning.

Honor is a very important issue to Muslim families, and it is within a woman's reach to bring dishonor on her whole family. As a result of this, women are "protected" from impurity and dishonor by staying close to the home, and taking the primary responsibility for managing the household.

Sexuality is suppressed among the feminine, whereas it tends to be more exercised by the men, depending on their individual devotion.

Unfortunately, in the darker corners of Islamic culture, there still exists a propensity to punish women for crimes perpetrated against them.   Sometimes physical abuse, and sometimes 'honor' killings. In these cases, the men related to a woman who was raped will injure or murder the woman in order to 'protect' the family from dishonor. These cases were most recently noted in media and print coverage of warfare in former Yugoslavia.

Although I don't know a single Muslim who would even imagine performing such an atrocity, it must be noted for the case of honesty. This may also give you a direction in which to focus your efforts and your prayer.

The Qur'an is explicit about how women should dress:

And say to the believing woman that they cast down their looks and guard their private parts and do not display their ornaments except what appears thereof, and let them wear their head-coverings over their bosoms, and not display their ornaments except to their husbands or their fathers, or the fathers' of their husbands, or their sons, or the sons of their husbands' or their brothers or their brothers' sons, or their sisters' sons, or their women, or those whom their right hands' possess, or the male servants not having need (of women), or the children who have not attained the knowledge of what is hidden in women; (Q 24:31 The Light)

However, the *ayat* prior to this one discusses the purity of *men,* and is only *two* lines long.

The head-covering and the accompanying veil are known as *abbaya,* or *hijab,* and in conservative Islamic States such as Saudi Arabia they are required. Punishment for disobedience of the law is severe, and is usually carried out by a male of the family in a display of devotion to Islam and to reclaim honor lost by the offender. In many Islamic states, the *abaya* is traditional, although not legally required.   In the west, it is an item of controversy, and if you befriend a Muslim woman in your city, you would be wise to make her feel comfortable with whatever decision she makes regarding traditions.

Muslim men traditionally fear western influence and corruption: keep that in mind if you intend to help "modernize" the beliefs of your Muslim friend.

Remember, as always, that the goal is to bring Jesus into your relationship with your Muslim friend, *not* westernism, materialism, postmodernism, feminism, capitalism, or any other -ism.

Half the value

In Islamic states, the legal evaluation of women is approximately half that of a man. It's an actual judicial stipulation, in court cases, for inheritance, and for compensation. A daughter receives half the entitlement as a son does, and so on and so forth. It takes the word of two women to counter that of a man in terms of testimony.

A woman is assumed to be of the religion of her husband. If a Muslim man marries a Christian woman, she is a Muslim. That is why Muslim men are permitted to marry from any religion, and Muslim women cannot marry outside their faith.

In countries that are ruled by the Sharia, it is illegal to convert from Islam to another religion, and often the penalty is death, for both the offender and the guilty proselyte.

Despite this, there are few Muslim women who have any deep understanding of Islam, and their homebound status as well as their disposition as "secondary-to-men" makes them typically hungry for friendship. Because Muslims honor purity, it is best if men befriend men and women befriend women, particularly when meeting in a home, or alone.

The Saudi princess

Just to show you that things aren't always the way you expect them to be, let me tell you a story.

My friend Frank (not his real name) came out to visit my wife and I in Beirut a few years back. We'd planned to stick around the house mostly, but we did have a short excursion planned to visit some friends in Saudi Arabia, and Frank and I had arranged to meet a Saudi princess through a mutual friend.

There are hundreds, if not thousands of people who are Saudi royalty, connected by generation and marriage to the house of Saud. These people are generally affluent members of society, and many of them are well traveled, and have some of the finest education available.

We met the princess at her home. She entertained us with the traditional tea, and we sat down to talk. There were, oh...I think six people present, and as usual, before long the conversation turned into the snakepit: politics. I *hate* talking about politics – somebody always gets hurt.

The princess had a unique perspective, however. She was a well educated, highly intelligent member of the royal class, and had a degree in journalism, of all things. Some of her work had been published in national presses, and she used her intellect and position to discuss women's rights, cultural instability, and the conflict between westernism and entrenched Islamic traditions. Despite these topics, she remained respectful of Islam, as it was the religion of her people, and she had a deep sense of offense at the west, America in particular.

So the conversation became strained. She became more vocal and adamant, delivering one criticism after another in her perfectly articulated English.

Frank and I just sat there, unsure of what to say. She was making her points very well, and yet, she seemed so genuinely angry at the west, we could tell it was a *personal* matter to her – not merely a political argument.

I hear a lot of arguments against the US; attacking our foreign policy and our national stance on the Israeli/Palestinian conflict. I have seen the rocks thrown, the flag burned in person - many times. Always, I have been able to observe these things with impunity because I understand the heart of the Arab people, and because I've made it my personal goal to withstand these differences so that I can make friends and talk about Jesus. It's never been a political issue to me – or a geographical one either. It's about the heart, and that's how I like it.

However, this anti-American monologue was so heated that even *I* was getting irritated. My palms were sweating, and my pulse was up around the point of no return.

And then Frank spoke up, "Look," he said, "there's one thing that's really obvious about all of this."

She stopped and looked at him, probably anticipating some retaliation, "what is that?"

"Well," Frank leaned forward on the sofa and put his elbows on his knees, "you've been hurt very badly, and I'm sorry for that, I really am."

"Excuse me?" She asked, taken back, "what do you mean?"

"Yes," I said, curious. I looked sideways at him, "what *do* you mean?"

"I can tell you're very intelligent. You've told us about your work in the Saudi news presses, and I know you're very knowledgeable about all the East vs. West conflicts. Christianity, politics, economics, women's rights, all of those things. But I can tell from listening to you for fifteen minutes, that your feelings on these issues don't come from your education or your work. They come from your heart."

She didn't know what to say.

Frank continued, and I heard the strain in his voice.

"Your heart, Princess, is wounded."

I looked over at him, and I saw a glint of moisture in his eyes. I couldn't believe it. We were in the middle of a heated discussion, and Frank was starting to cry. He was getting compassionate, and I was getting angry.

Right then, I knew: Frank was doing what *Jesus* does. He was looking at the heart – with compassion. I prayed inside, *dear Jesus, help me to see what you see.*

The princess broke. She leaned forward on the couch and sobbed.

After a few minutes, she looked up, and wiped her eyes, "you are right; I am hurt, and I see no way out of it. I'm trapped in the layers of politics and religion and culture." She stopped, "I have spent all of my life to find some meaning, something to belong to, and it always circulates back to the same old things. It's so disappointing. I try to reach the people of Saudi Arabia to give them hope, and I have no hope myself."

Frank nodded. "I understand."

"Let me ask you a question, if I may," I said.

She nodded, "of course."

"What if I told you that there was a kingdom that was much larger than Saudi Arabia, much greater than America, much deeper than the culture of Europe, and much richer than either than the religious institutions of Christianity or Islam. What would you say to that?"

The princess looked over her shoulder toward her uncle who was standing in the corner of the room. Because of the traditions and the deep reverence for Islam, we had to be wary – the slightest hint of irreverence would bring our conversation to an end. The anticipation in the room heightened palpably for a moment.

Her uncle nodded, with discernment displayed on his bearded face. He seemed to know that we meant no harm.

I continued, "would you be interested in a kingdom of hope?"

"Certainly," she said, "does God offer this hope?"

"Yes," I said, "he does, and he has made a gateway to it – an entrance to this kingdom."

She looked suspicious for a moment, "are you trying to tell me that I should convert to Christianity?"

"No." I held up my hand for a moment, "Princess, what does the word 'Muslim' mean to you?"

"Well…," she thought for a moment, "in the traditional sense, it means 'submitted'."

"I understand, highness," I said, "but what does it mean to you? What do you want it to mean?"

She shook her head, "I'm not sure what you're saying."

Frank picked up seamlessly where I left off, "Princess, what if 'submitted' could mean 'to belong to'? You spoke to us about hope, about significance, about meaning. If you can find these things with Allah, in this kingdom, would you not be the truest form of 'Muslim'? Would you not truly be submitted to God?"

"Do I have to change my beliefs?" She asked, "because this is not tradition: God is aloof, he is unknown by men."

"But he *is* known by men. And by women. He has made this kingdom available."

"He has?" she asked, "is it paradise? Our reward in death?"

"Princess," I leaned forward on the sofa, looking her in the eyes, "it is here, right now."

She looked over her shoulder at her uncle again. He again nodded, and I could see in his eyes that he was a man of deep understanding. If we had come in preaching, he would have seen through us in a second, but he seemed to be aware of the fact that we were genuine.

"How can I have this kingdom?"

"Allah sent a prophet. The Qur'an tells us that he is the *word of God*, that he is a spirit from God, and that he sits close to God. His name is Isa, and he is near to God now."

She nodded, "you call him *Isa al-Mesiah*, Jesus the Messiah."

"Yes," I said, "and since both of our holy books say that he was the word of God, and a spirit from God, we have spent our lives following him, belonging to his kingdom."

"How do you belong to his kingdom?" She asked.

"The first thing that Isa preached was that the kingdom of heaven is at hand." I said.

"Is it?" she asked.

"I believe it is," I said, "I believe that you can have this kingdom, and I believe you will find the kind of hope that you long for, the kind of peace you write about. I believe that to be truly submitted to Allah is to be with him in spirit, in his kingdom, and I believe that Isa can open that door for you because he is near to Allah."

She gave another glance at her uncle. "Can we pray to Allah and ask him to speak to us about his kingdom?"

And we did. Frank and I took turns asking for God to reveal his kingdom to our new friend, that she could be filled with God's hope and peace, and that she could see Isa for who he really was to her.

This story illustrates a few interesting points, but I ought to let you know: very few Muslim women are royalty. Very few Muslims *people* at all, actually. It doesn't always work like this.

Many Muslim women are captivated by fear, superstition, and the belief that because they are less valuable on earth, they are also less valuable to God.

A Christ-like perspective

Labels and their meanings

As you read that last story, I'm sure that a few red flags were raised. That's okay – hopefully you're still reading this.

This is what I'm getting at: the definitions and labels aren't important. *The heart is.* Jesus has different names in every culture. The word 'God' is different in almost every language. Strangely, the western church model has quite literally spent centuries changing the name tags and labels in every continent of the globe, 'converting' people to 'Christianity' rather than turning people's hearts toward their creator, whatever name he goes by.

A friend of mine illustrated this point to me asking, "what if I told you that Jesus was the pig of God?"

My jaw dropped, "I'd be a little offended," I said, "that's contrary to scripture."

"Of course, but, try telling that to a primitive tribe in Indonesia."

"What do you mean?" I asked.

"It's an illustration I had to use once," he said, "they don't have sheep in Indonesia, so I had no way to explain the sacrifice of Jesus for their sins, other than to use a wild pig as an example instead."

It hit me then – *it was the reality of the sacrifice*, not the textbook verbiage that mattered.

"What, do you think we'd have to import sheep into every people group on the planet before we tell them the good news about Jesus?" he asked with a laugh.

He was right. And in the same way, we don't have to import *our* culture and our religious traditions and labels to tell people about Jesus. Jesus is compatible with every culture because he *is* the gospel, and he gives himself freely. Jesus looks for a change of heart; men look for a change of culture.

It's always a matter of the heart – and Jesus can do that work *on his own*.

Back to my point: women and Islam. Women are expected to practice the teachings of the faith, although they are considered Muslim by marriage anyway. The monthly period is believed to nullify the prayers and fasting given during the time of the period, however.

A way to build rapport with a Muslim woman is to talk about *her* life, her heart, her experiences, and her beliefs. Too often the conversation turns westward as the Muslim woman is curious about life as an American or European woman. If we're truly living the model set by Jesus Christ, we should make any and every attempt to make our assertions, questions, and compassion about the other person, not about us and our western lives. Be real, but don't let the conversation turn into "how the west is better for women" because that isn't the point. The point is that Jesus loves women as much as he does men. Use the stories of Jesus to point this out: Mary Magdalene, the Samaritan woman, the woman caught in adultery, the woman with the perfume vial, and the story of Mary sitting at Jesus' feet while Martha prepared the meal. Jesus himself said, "There is only one thing necessary, and Mary has chosen the good part. What she has will not be taken away from her."

Jesus enjoyed Mary's company, and there are many Muslim women who he longs to sit and be with.

V. A FRACTURED FAMILY

ISLAM AND CONFLICT

The problem of peace

Our western outlook for some time now has been one that is unbalanced, and it's easy to see why. From the Pan-Am flight bombing that decimated a passenger aircraft over Lockerbie, Scotland, to the bombing of the Marine barracks in my adopted home-town of Beirut, to the terrorist attacks of 9/11, we have seen brutality and hatred.

Whether we do so deliberately or not, we often choose to believe that the problem is Islam itself. Although there is no doubt that religion in and of itself is a hotbed for deep convictions, zealous emotions and, at times, fiery conflicts, there is nothing conclusive gained by accusing the religion itself of brokering the violence committed by a handful of its followers.

Christine Mallouhi points out that: "Real Christians, Muslims, and Jews do not murder. Terrorists murder and terrorists do not discriminate for *a terrorist's religion is hate and terror.*"[ii] (Italics mine.)

I agree. Too often I have heard one person or another, fed up with the problem of international terrorism, say something as in, "it's time we quit making excuses for them and just call a spade a spade." Usually, people like this have the misunderstanding that murder and Islam are synonymous.

So I typically return with: "you're absolutely right. Murderers are murderers, and we should stop making excuses for them."

I have lived and loved and shared and grieved with Muslims for over twenty years. In the few acts of violence I have encountered, I have never *once* seen a radical terrorist live in accordance with any real standard of values; Muslim, Christian, or otherwise. People who kill other people in order to create fear and subservience are called one thing: evil. It is simply not accurate or fair to insist that Muslims are terrorists, any more than it is to say that the cause of communism is Russian people.

Unfortunately, the western outlook is quick to point to the religion of Islam itself as the point of origin without a wider understanding of the brutal history of conflict between what have been labeled as the "three great monotheisms." Judaism was attributed to Abraham and Moses, Christianity was born by people who were attempting to follow the revolutionary life, death and resurrection of Jesus Christ. Hundreds of years later, Islam was born with a claim to the Arab lineage: Ishmael, the son of Hagar, Abraham's first offspring. Due to the overlap between these three monotheistic beliefs, there has been a blatantly conflicted history in which men of all three religions have murdered, stolen, pillaged, and burned – all in the name of the God of the same lineage – the God of Abraham.

At various points throughout our shared history, wars, politics, and religious zeal for God and Real Estate has brought the three religions which are normally peaceful into the campaign stages, where popes, prophets, priests and people began to beat their plowshares back into swords for what Christendom called "Holy war" and Islam called "Jihad."

Palestine: power and...peace?

I may be biased, but it seems that we in the west have pledged allegiance to the nation of Israel, at the expense of its Arab neighbors. Much of this reason is surely due to the fact that Israel suffered so brutally during the Nazi years. Our compassion has encouraged us to stand behind the Jewish people as they rightly seek a homeland. And many of the returning Israelis have been our very own neighbors. Finally, our shared historical and theological/biblical heritage provides a natural bridge with our Jewish friends.

Unfortunately, we have sometimes taken this too far. Does God love one people at the expense of others? Amazingly, I have often heard comments from the pulpit proclaiming the virtues of the nation-state of Israel while at the same time encouraging the virtual extermination of the Palestinian Arabs attempting to share the same land. Does God honestly need our political help to fulfill his plan for all peoples? If, in fact, Israel should exist on the current land, is it at the cost of Jesus' compassion?

Let's not forget God's promise to Abraham that "through you **ALL** the nations of the earth will be **BLESSED**."

I remember as a child that communism was very much the same fixated enemy of both the state and the church. If you were sympathetic to the Soviet empire, then you were castigated as a non-Christian, and your friends, family, and church went out of their way to avoid you. Now, it seems that Islam has taken the hot seat vacated by the demise of the cold war.

Dr. King speaks

Just to make a point, I found one of Martin Luther King Jr.'s speeches, and I made a simple substitution. I replaced the words "communism" and "communist" with the appropriate substitutions "Islamic Fundamentalism" and "terrorism," just to see where Dr. King would stand on the issue if he was alive today and held the Crescent and Scimitar in the same esteem as the Hammer and the Sickle.

If in any way I misrepresent Dr. King, the fault is mine, and I mean no offense by it.

"Finally, we are challenged to dedicate our lives to the cause of Christ even as the [Islamic Fundamentalists] dedicate theirs to [Islamic Fundamentalism]. We who cannot accept the creed of the [Fundamentalists] recognize their zeal and commitment to a cause which they believe will create a better world. They have a sense of purpose and destiny, and they work passionately and assiduously to win others to [Islamic Fundamentalism]. How many Followers of Jesus are as concerned to win others for Christ? Often we have neither zeal for Christ nor zest for his kingdom. For so many who bear the name of Christ, "Christianity" is a Sunday activity bearing no relevancy for Monday and the church is little more than a secular social club having a thin veneer of religiosity. Jesus is an ancient symbol whom we do the honor of calling Christ, and yet his Lordship is neither affirmed nor acknowledged by our substance-less lives. Would that our fire were burning in the hearts of all who follow Christ with the same intensity as the [Muslim Fundamentalists'] fire is burning within their hearts! Is this brand of [Islam] alive in the world today because we have not been Christ-centered enough?

"We need to pledge ourselves anew to the cause of Christ. We must recapture the spirit of the early believers. Wherever the early disciples went, they made a triumphant witness for Christ. Whether on the village streets or in the city jails, they daringly proclaimed the good news of the gospel. Their reward for this audacious witness was often the excruciating agony of a lion's den or the poignant pain of a chopping block, but they continued in the faith that they had discovered a cause so great and had been transformed by a Savior so divine that even death was not too great a sacrifice. When they entered a town, the power structure became disturbed. Their new gospel brought the refreshing warmth of spring to men whose lives had been hardened by the long winter of traditionalism. They urged men to revolt against the old systems of injustice and the old structures of immorality. When the rulers objected, these strange people, intoxicated by the wine of God's grace, continued to proclaim the gospel until even men and women in Caesar's household were convinced, until jailers dropped their keys, and until kings trembled on their thrones. T.R. Glover has written that the early Followers of Jesus "out-thought, out-lived, and out-died" everyone else.

"Where is that fervor today? Where is that kind of daring, revolutionary commitment to Christ today? Is it hidden behind smoke screens and altars? Is it buried in a grave called respectability? Is it inextricably bound within nameless status quos and imprisoned within cells of stagnant mores? This devotion must again be released. Christ must once more be enthroned in our lives.

"This is our best defense against [terrorism]. War is not the answer. [Terrorism] will never be defeated by the use of atomic bombs or nuclear weapons. Let us not join those who shout war and through who their misguided passions urge the United States to relinquish its participation in the United Nations. These are the days when people who follow Jesus must evince wise restraint and calm reasonableness. We must not call everyone a [Fundamentalist Muslim] or an appeaser who recognizes that hate and hysteria are not the final answers to the problems of these turbulent days. We must not engage in a negative anti-[Muslim] campaign, but rather in a positive thrust for democracy, realizing that our greatest defense against [terrorism] is to take offensive action in behalf of justice and righteousness. After our condemnation of the philosophy of [Islamic Fundamentalism] has been eloquently expressed, we must with positive action seek to remove those conditions of poverty, insecurity, injustice, and racial discrimination which are the fertile soil in which the seeds of all kinds of [Fundamentalism] grows and develops. [Islamic Fundamentalism] thrives only when the doors of opportunity are closed and human aspirations are stifled. Like the early disciples, we must move into a sometimes hostile world armed with the revolutionary gospel of Jesus Christ. With this powerful gospel we shall boldly challenge the status quos and unjust mores and thereby speed the day when "every valley shall be exalted, and every mountain and hill shall be made low; and the crooked shall be made straight. The rough places plain,; and the glory of the Lord shall be revealed.

"Our hard challenge and our sublime opportunity is to bear witness to the spirit of Christ in fashioning a truly Christ-centered world. If we accept the challenge with devotion and valor, the bell of history will toll for [Islamic fundamentalism] and [terrorism]. And we shall make the world safe for democracy and secure for the people of Christ."[iii]

I hope you'll forgive me if you feel that I'm using Dr. King in a merely self-serving manner, but I thought it might make an interesting point. Obviously, it doesn't fit in every mold perfectly: the references to democracy and the United Nations may not be apropos to the context of sharing good news with our Muslim friends, but I think that on the whole we can learn a lot as western Christians regarding our perspective on Islam; and Dr. King is, in my opinion, a man who was every bit as good as his word, a man who lived by his beliefs, and led from the front.

To quote another notable follower of Christ, the late Mother Teresa of Calcutta:

"We all have the duty to serve God where we are called to do so. I feel called to serve individuals, to love each human being. My calling is *not to judge the institutions. I am not qualified to condemn anyone.* I never think in terms of a crowd, but of individual persons.

If I thought in terms of crowds, I would never begin my work.

I believe in the personal touch of one to one.

If others are convinced that God wants them to change social structures, *that is a matter for them to take up with God."*[iv]

(Italics mine)

65

It goes without saying that if you want to reach a person; you have to look at them as an *individual*. The preconceptions that you may have about Islam need to be discarded from the beginning if you want to have a genuine relationship with a Muslim. There can be no more generalizations and blanket distinctions.

Mother Teresa's exhortation to base the gospel from the "…personal touch of one to one…" echoes the wisdom and compassion of Jesus, who while he was busy, surrounded by mobs of people, *continually* took the time to touch individual people, with healing, forgiveness, admonition, and salvation.

I know that to the west, America in particular, my perspective regarding the Palestinian conflict may be viewed as ignorant or unjust. I do not, in any way, believe that the existence of an Israeli State is *questionable*. I do not "hold a side" when it comes to geopolitical distinctions, and I do not believe that any person, Muslim/Arab or Israeli has the right to bomb, shoot, burn, or defile the people and/or presence of another culture in order to gain religious or political dominance. War is always a tragedy.

My point is that the Christian school of thought often holds an unjust scale, weighing allegiance to Jesus versus allegiance to a political group or nation. The very idea that a Christian should call for the destruction of Muslim people is absolutely contrary to the perspective of Jesus, who healed Arab and Jew alike.

Cousins in conflict

The earliest division within Islam itself happened two decades after Muhammad died. When Muhammad's son-in-law, Ali, became the fourth caliph (spiritual/cultural leader within Islam), he was not universally accepted because he was not the son of Muhammad by blood, but by marriage. Ali was assassinated, and his sons, in turn took up the fight. *Hassan* was murdered by poisoning, and *Hussein* died in combat ten years later.

The party of Ali (Shi'a Ali) became known as the Shi'a, or Shi'ite sect, and today they comprise only about ten percent of the Muslim world, primarily in Iran, as well as a growing demographic of Shi'a Islam in Iraq.

The primary difference between Sunni and Shi'a is that the Shi'ites believe that Ali was the first actually rightful caliph. Today, the word *Imam* is used.

These Imams are directly descended from Ali himself, and are considered righteous and, to some, even infallible. They do not recognize any Imam who is outside of the bloodline of Ali, and they even commemorate the martyrdom of Hussein, which is quite a festival.

By and large, the Shi'a sect believes in the logical adaptation of Islamic Law, for instance, contextualization, and more appropriate measures rather than the rigid line of Sharia.

Sunni Muslims constitute the vast majority of mainstream Islam, from the more contemporary nominal Muslim population to some of the most brutal and repressive dictatorships in the world. They do not hold the belief that the imamate line of Shi'a Ali is the solely legitimate source of Muslim leadership, and in countries where Sharia is enforced, it is considered to be immutable, and to change it would be to break it – bringing strict consequences.

Sunni Islam typically oppresses its minority Shi'a cousin, through persecution, political superiority, and in some cases, outright bloodshed, most notably in Iraq some years prior to the recent U.S./British led invasion.

From 1979 on, under Saddam Hussein, the ruling Baath party (secular Sunni) persecuted the Shi'ites of southern Iraq with the same ferocity as they persecuted the Kurdish people of the north.

The great majority of Muslims are people who are like you and me: they want to have a safe and peaceful life with their family and their friends. Less than five percent of Islamic adherents practice extremism, or even believe in it.

This faction of Islam is what constitutes the members of such groups as the Taliban, The Muslim Brotherhood, and the Wahhabi sect of Saudi Arabia.

Sons of Abraham

This is something of a misnomer here in the west. Christians consider the inheritance and lineage of Abraham to be a spiritual birthright, even according to the apostle Paul. In reality, very few western Christians are actually *biologically* related at all to the Abrahamic bloodline. Not that I'm picking on the term; I believe it to be a spiritual reality – God told Abraham that all the nations of the earth would be blessed though him, and here we are today, partakers in the Kingdom of God because, in part, the obedience of Abraham.

What is ironic is the view that many western Christians tend to have toward Islam, believing it to be illegitimate. The widespread Christian perspective for some time has been that because Islam was founded on the coattails of Judaism and Christianity, it is not genuine, and its Arabian roots are not in fact really of Abraham at all.

Christians however, tend to have a more favorable view of Judaism because it is part and parcel of the faith to the same One True God. We view ours through messianic extension, we view Judaism as the older traditions of the same, and all too often we disregard Islam offhandedly as a fake, and by doing so, we injure people and mock the sincerity of their faith. I am not suggesting that all three monotheistic faiths are the same – I'm merely pointing out that every Muslim believes that his religion is also directly connected to Abraham. Why argue this point? Faith in Abraham is not the issue.

The last twenty-plus years of foreign policy here in the United States have shown a clear favoritism toward the state of Israel while cold-shouldered foreign policy often relegates Arabs to the corner. I am sad to say, these policies do not exist solely for policy's sake: they exist by constituency, the opinions of the populace. American people are to blame in many ways, myself included. Our legislative, executive, and even our military/intelligence policies and practices toward the Arab world have often been born out of fear, ignorance, and prejudice. Instead of blaming our elected representatives, we should first seek to find the log which is in our own eye by taking responsibility for any anti-Arab/anti-Muslim tendencies which live within our hearts, our communities, and our nations. If we were to truly believe that "perfect love casts out fear," then we should not allow fear to cause us to disregard, spurn, or attack those who are different.

There is so much fear of the unknown faith of the Muslim, that we often credit all of Islam with the violence of the few. By foreign policy we sometimes create tensions and add "insult to injury" to the Muslim sense of honor, which runs very deep.

I think a part of this rift is due to western influence, although there certainly have been long and lasting tensions through the heart of Palestine itself.

Let me make two important qualifications:
1. If you already have an extremely strong sense of bias for Israel and against its Islamic neighbors, then this book will not do much good for you. My intention here is not to make a final and adamant exposition for equality. If you're not capable of that on your own, then no book will help. I merely want to point out that *many of us do have* a prejudice, and that Jesus had

no prejudice in his heart toward any. If we are at all serious about making Muslim friends we must begin by dropping the issue of policy and Israeli/Palestinian conflict. It's not about that – don't let it be.

2. Muslims are wounded people, injured by the stigma attached to them because of radical movements. They have the same fear of Christians that Christians do of them. Because of the thousand-plus years of division and fighting between the Big Three monotheisms, there are plenty of hot buttons and landmines in your heart as well as your friends' heart. Touchy spots, places of past irritation. Make an earnest decision not to be defensive, retaliatory, or presumptuous. It is about you, your friend, and Jesus, not about the big institutions and the history of hatred and shame.

A Christ-like perspective

Be Thou Fruity

The whole idea behind "bearing fruit" is relationship. Like a tree or any other living thing, relationships are key to fruitfulness.

On a tree, the leaves have a photosynthetic relationship with the sun. The roots have a complex hydration system. The trunk grows in proportion to environment: temperature, wind, exposure.

Having said that, look at your method of evangelism. Do you preach on the streets? Do you pass out tracts or go door to door? Do you sit on a barstool and tell your drinking buddies about God?

Take a long look, and I'll give you some pointers.

The first one is: forget evangelism as a methodology. You know how it feels when somebody approaches you with a religious angle. You don't like having evangelism "done" to you, so I don't advise "doing evangelism" to others.

Make it about building a true friendship and let Christ change the heart. Simply present Jesus. Be interested, participate, ask questions, and above all, love and respect your friend. This method is called discipleship or mentoring. You don't start with a list of doctrines that need to be believed in order to convert, you start with simple friendship. Always assume that your friend is more devoted than you, not less. I always tell my friends, "Boy, when I have my life as wholesome as yours, I'll have it made." They laugh, but it makes a point: I'm not assuming I'm better than them simply because I like talking about Jesus. If you act as if they are a sinner, you won't be around them for very long.

Discipleship is the sum of time spent with somebody, not about the sinner's prayer or the end result. And discipleship is the root concept of Matthew 28:19, the great commission:

"Go and make disciples of all nations…"

VI. ALL THE RIGHT QUESTIONS

MUSLIMS WANT TO KNOW ABOUT JESUS

Curiosity has its merits

Here I've compiled the top five questions that my Muslim friends ask me. My point is *not* to hand out talking points for theological rebuttal, but rather to give you more insight into the typical questions you will encounter with Muslims who are eager to talk about God, Jesus, and the holy books.

1. Do you believe the Qur'an is God's inspired book?

I always *encourage* my Muslim friends to read the Qur'an. This is because many Muslims are aware of the structure of Islam from tradition rather than close study, and many have never read the Qur'an. When they do, it leads many of them to a series of questions, and because the Qur'an encourages Muslims to read the Gospels, I often see fruit that comes from encouraging this devotion. However, if one of your Muslim friends blatantly asks you, "is the Qur'an a holy book from God?" you have a theologically heavy issue to deal with. Don't take the question lightly – it is extremely important to a Muslim. There are two ways to look at the question before you answer it:

First, you should realize that the Qur'an would never have been written unless God allowed it to be written. Although some might view this approach as a dodge around the "real" issue, I would challenge them to think deeper: Look at the

Qur'an as a book which can propel people to become curious about Jesus. I stress this always, because Jesus *is* the way, and any method or way to come to him is legitimate if the seeker actually finds Christ as the answer to the soul's burning need. Even Jesus, when his disciples found a man casting out demons and healing people without his sanction, approved it, because he knew that there was *no other name by which people could be saved.* (Acts 4:12)

Another ordinary way to view this issue is to actually examine the veracity of the Qur'an, which means that you have to read it for yourself. While this can be time-consuming, it will give you rewards in terms of your friendships because you will have acquired the credibility you need to talk effectively about the Qur'an. And there's no way you can make a decision regarding it's veracity without being knowledgeable enough to do so anyway. At the very least, you will have read a book highly revered by a fifth of the earth's population!

The final option would be to simply deny any supernatural credence to the Qur'an right up front. Which I don't recommend. There are no long-term benefits in doing so, and "winning" that point may cost in the long run. Again, the rule of thumb – be sensitive. Remember, that the concept of holiness is different to a Muslim, and this concept is at least deserving of respect.

2. Do you believe Muhammad is a true prophet of God?

Again, think this question through before you make a knee-jerk reaction. Ask yourself, "what is a prophet, anyway?" I believe it's important to verify *every* self-claimed prophet, whether they're in your church or in a mosque.

Here's my advice: recognize that Muhammad wanted his people to return to the one true God, and respect that tradition. But don't get caught in a debate about Muhammad.

Always move back toward common ground: Jesus. Base your position on the things Muhammad said about Jesus, instead of making an opposition based on the differences. Later on, I know it is logical to wonder where and how the teachings differed, and to want to try to argue them, but I believe that there are many customs, traditions, and practices that we can have respect for *while* we begin to explain the good news of Jesus.

3. Has the Bible been changed?

This is a common belief, and one that is commonly taught among Muslims. Many Muslims believe that God revealed himself to the Israelites and later to the Christians, and yet, the "people of the book" changed and distorted the teachings of God, and as such, the Bible of the Christians can be misleading.

There are ways to deal with this. Rather than defense, I think it is better to bring all of the relevant material back to Jesus, and keep the discussion there, because Jesus reveals truth.

If however, you are at a point in your relationship where you feel it is the right time to begin pushing the boundaries, then you should begin by pointing out what the Qur'an itself says about the Bible.

Interestingly enough, there are several verses within the Qur'an which seem to indicate the opposite of the claims that the Bible has "been changed."

The *Taureh* was given to Moses by God, the *Zabur* was given to David by God, and the *Injeel* was given to Jesus the Messiah by God. In any case, there are numerous references where the Qur'an says of itself that it is a confirmation of the book that "…was before it" – the Bible.

"We [God] gave to Moses the Book and after him sent succeeding Messengers." (Q 2:87)

"Indeed, We gave Moses the Book; so be not in doubt concerning the encounter with him; and We appointed it for a guidance to the Children of Israel." (Q 32:23)

"..And we gave unto David the Psalms." (Q 4:163)

"And We sent, following Isa the son of Marium, and We gave unto him the Injeel [gospel]." (Q 57:27)

"This is a Book [the Qur'an] We have sent down, blessed and confirming that which was before it [the Bible]." (Q 6:92)

4.   How can God have a son?

This is a *cornerstone* difficulty that you will face: Muslims believe in Jesus, but not that he was the son of God, and it is tempting for us to simply say: "Jesus is who he said he was."

There are various venerable and accurate ways to do this, but once again, *is this really the point?*

Jesus is the point. Not the things *about* Jesus!

Interestingly, Jesus is referred to in the Qur'an itself as "Isa the Messiah," and "Isa the Christ."

Muslims believe that it is a serious transgression to make any person equivalent with God, and the concept of the trinity (which many Muslims believe consists in the 'Christian' mind as God, Mary, and Jesus) is sacrilegious.

To the Muslim, the idea of Jesus being transferred to earth as a "word from God," or a "spirit from heaven," is normal – that's what the Qur'an teaches. But the idea of God having relations with a human woman to produce an offspring is ludicrous and blasphemy. (Which is what many think we mean when we say "Son of God").

It often works to simply explain that this is not what the Bible teaches. God was not a man with a baby boy named "Jesus." One of Jesus' titles is the "Son of God." This was a title given to kings in the Old Testament and may have more to do with his Kingship than it does his relationship with the Father. (Although it clearly cannot be disputed that there was a deep father/son relationship at the core of Jesus' ministry, as seen in John 17:24)

5. Was he crucified?

For a Muslim, it is against God's nature, or even his capability to allow such a prophet to be killed by human hands. It is believed that God was 'above' the execution of Jesus by tricking the Jews and the Romans into *believing* that he'd been crucified. At the same time, Muslims believe that Jesus ascended to God, and that at the end times he will come to earth, be killed, and then raised to life again.

It is interesting to note that some recent studies of the Qur'an point to the fact that the Qur'an *does*, in fact, say that Jesus did (or will) die.

Let me explain my thoughts on this topic by telling a story. Several years ago in downtown Beirut, I was meeting with a group of Muslim businessmen and political leaders in one of their homes. We were in the middle of an interesting and vibrant discussion about Jesus in the gospel of Luke, when a visitor walked in. He was someone I had never met, but was a friend of the others. After realizing what we were doing, he said in shock, "But we're Muslims. How can you be talking about Jesus with *that man*?" He pointed at me, "he believes that Jesus was crucified and we do not," he concluded.

All heads turned towards me to see my reaction. In years past I would have reverted to an apologetic approach; explaining to our new friend that indeed the Bible does teach that Jesus died and rose again and that he should believe that too in order to obtain eternal life. But what I did instead surprised even me. I looked at him, smiled and shrugged my shoulders, lifting my hands up as if to say, "sorry; what's your point?"

Immediately all of my other friends came to the rescue of this awkward silence by turning on their friend with an adamant rebuttal.

"Yeah, why did you have to bring *that* up? We were having a nice discussion about Jesus before you came in!" The visitor sat down with a sigh and we continued reading through Luke.

Now, you may be asking, do *I* think it's important for my Muslim friends to know and understand the death and resurrection of Jesus Christ? Of course! Vital. But we often forget that Jesus died at the *end* of his life, not the beginning. We do present "Christ and him crucified" but not necessarily on day one. Let the story be just that – a story. It has a beginning, a middle and an end.

I often like to say to my friends in the Muslim world, "Let's talk about Jesus. Let's discuss his life, his teachings, his ways. When we get to that hard part about whether he died or not – well, we'll deal with that then." In the right time. In the right way.

A Christ-like perspective

Embrace the questions

The first step is one of immense self-control and a deep desire to present Jesus to your Muslim friend: drop the arguments, and forget the fight. It isn't about who's *more* right and who's *more* wrong. It's about pointing toward Isa (Jesus) and allowing his Spirit to do the heavy lifting.

Take the questions you receive seriously. They are not mere discussions, they are articles of faith. Muslims believe in divinity to a fault – they will sacrifice themselves in an argument in order to uphold the sovereignty of God, and they do not accept anything which lessens God's greatness. God is unimpeachable in his greatness.

This gives you a tremendously good opportunity. You can always be respectful and even religious with the questions and topics of discussion while simultaneously being genuine and enthusiastic about Jesus.

Ask questions yourself. But don't pry. You can gain the respect of your friend by showing that you are a seeker also. Engage your friend with questions that give you both something to think about

VII. STANDING ON THE BRIDGE

MUSLIMS WHO FOLLOW JESUS

Heresy

The most serious heresy in Islam is to leave Islam. Those who do are often abandoned, ostracized, cut off, and in some places, executed. To leave the path of God for anything is to invoke his wrath, and Muslims live in fear of this, which is where some of their devotion comes from.

As a result of this, I have begun to follow some specific guidelines for talking to my Muslim friends about Jesus, and the first thing I do is toss out the "gospel of terminology".

Case in point:

"I'm still a Muslim, though," one of my friends said to me when I asked him if following Jesus meant that he had become a Christian.

"Oh?" I said, curious.

"Yes," Ahmad said, "I am a Muslim who follows Jesus."

"How does *that* work?" I asked him, "what does your family think of that?"

"They think nothing of it," he looked at me strangely, "I am a Muslim, what should they think?"

I had to think about that for a minute, and then it hit me: accepting Jesus as his teacher had taught him to make Jesus his leader, and in turn, it had taken him to the revelation of who Jesus *really was*. At no point had Jesus ever said to my friend, "you must change your name, go to a western church, give up your family and tribe, and become a republican."

Instead, Jesus said the same two words to Ahmad that he'd said to a couple of men in the same region about two thousand years ago: *"follow me."*

.

Hope

Truth be told, there are a growing number of Muslims around the world who maintain their cultural identity as "Muslim", but choose to align themselves with the spiritual and moral teachings of Jesus, becoming *his* disciples while becoming what "Muslim" truly means: submitted to God.

I know that there is quite a bit of controversy over this issue. Some of you who read this may find the concept to be a disagreeable one.

So we need to ask three basic questions:

1. Is it *theologically* viable for a Muslim to refer to himself as "follower of Jesus" and still be a Muslim?
2. Is it *culturally* feasible for a Muslim to remain a Muslim and follow Jesus?
3. Is there a need to become a "christian" in *terminology* in order to follow Jesus in both theological and cultural fashion?

We need to know if it lines up with the scriptures, the teachings of Jesus himself; and if it will actually work in the Muslim culture. The last question is the least, but it may be a bit of a pill for some people to swallow, and that is, is the terminology of Christendom important or not?

First of all, in the context of history, the issue is a major one. If a Muslim becomes a "Christian", the rejection will be immediate and final. If a Muslim can retain his cultural identity, and yet follow Jesus without having to convert his religious *title* to "Christianity" he benefits in that he can keep his family and his normal healthy relationships, as well as being able to begin what I like to call an "insider movement towards Jesus as Christ."

There are some historical instances which seem to be exceptions to this long-standing rejection of Jesus as anything other than a prophet.

I was recently reading my friends Christine's book, *Waging Peace on Islam,* which I've quoted already in this book (it's a mainstay in my personal library) when I came across a chapter entitled THE MYSTICAL INFLUENCE IN ISLAM. The following segment is drawn from Christine's work. When I read this, I was immediately surprised by what I found. Christine addressed the *Sufi* Muslims, who were monks who actually lived in exclusion from what they viewed as a widespread corruption of Islam.

Many of them lived in intentional poverty, nourishing the things of the Spirit, and many of them were completely dedicated to living according to the teachings of Jesus.

I was fascinated by this, fascinated by the way Jesus' wisdom and compassion had managed to find their way into the very heart of Islam.

The Sufi's believed that to serve God was to love God, purely and simply. They rigorously expended themselves in songs and dances, in pure worship of this creator God who made them so that they could live in a love relationship with him. They believed that all else was nothingness, a waste.

One mystic, a woman named Rabia Al Adawiyya (713-801) once said, "If I worship you [God] for fear of hell, burn me in hell." She firmly believed that God should not be loved out of fear, but rather because he was worthy of her love, and that he was beautiful. Christine wrote, "she longed to die in order to meet God."

(As a side, note, the Sufi's were one of the first sects of any religion to recognize the equality of men and women. Women could be Sufis, and could also be teachers or leaders over men.)

Another Sufi, named Ibn Al Arabi, was loved by many and hated by more. He remains today, one of the greatest of all Muslim thinkers. He believed that Jesus was the word, the spirit, and the servant of God. Even God's mouthpiece. He once wrote, "The person who catches the disease of Christ can never be cured."

Yet another, Jalal Al Din Al Rumi, used his own interpretation of the ritual ablutions before prayer by saying, "Lord wash me. My hand has washed this part of me, but my hand cannot wash my spirit. I can wash this skin, but you must wash me."

This flies directly against the typical Muslim concept of religion, in which the works of the flesh are critically significant. Rumi also believed that he could worship God in a Christian church, a Jewish synagogue or a Muslim mosque because, as he put it, "I see one altar."

One Sufi was martyred for heresy because of such convictions. He said "On the supreme example of the Cross I intend to die. For I seek neither the Batha (Mecca) nor the Medina."

This mystic's name was Hussein Ibn Mansour Hallaj. He was tortured, burned, crucified and dismembered for being a secret Christian in the eyes of his contemporaries. While he was tortured, he cried out, "by killing me you give me new life."

So the question is, would Jesus require a Muslim to "convert" to Christianity?

In all actuality, Jesus never actually used the word "Christian.". For that matter, neither did Paul. Peter did once, and it was in reference to the derogatory nature of the term. It appears one other time in the book of Acts, where someone called them the "Christians in Antioch."

We are never commanded, exhorted, or encouraged to use the word "Christian." It is, after all, a word, and for that matter a loaded word, filled with hidden meanings and historical grievances. A much better phrase, one which I use myself is: "follower of Jesus." This defines. It explains. It's dynamic and it's real. We really *are* following Jesus.

The reality is that Jesus was a Palestinian Jew, born of God and man, a thorn in the side of the religious community, all the while developing a grassroots followership, for which he died in order to sacrifice himself for their sins.

It then follows that his personal mission was not to found a new religion called "Christianity" but rather to, as he said, "seek and save the lost."

So however we define this , we can agree that his identity, at least in his teaching and lifestyle, was not "Christian."

We can actually see that the origin of the word may have actually been derogatory, as in Antioch where they were first *called* "little Christ's." . This is similar to a republican calling a democrat a "Clinton-ite" or in the opposite sense, "A Bush boy" identifying the individual with their beliefs in a snide and accusatory manner.

Paul pushes it even further. He stated in his letter to the Galatians that "there is neither Jew nor Gentile...for those who are in Christ," showing us that the obligatory cultural terminology does not carry any weight in the eyes of God. Those who are in Christ are in Christ, those who are not, simply aren't.

Fear not, Fear God

I want to close this chapter with a point which I hope will guide you and keep you. It can empower you, teach you, and above all, give you confidence in the eyes of the world and in the eyes of God.

First of all, there is the greatest commandment: love God and love people.   Love has always been and will always be the strongest force in the universe. No one can stand against it. Not the worst Muslim, nor the best Christian. It is who God is and who he wants us to be. Love. (See 1 john 4:7-8)

But there is something more. Read through the first chapter of Joshua to see what God commanded the children of Israel about fear.

"Be strong and courageous, and **do not fear.**"

And Jesus himself, in the gospels said, "Do not fear those who can kill you, but fear He who can destroy the body and soul in hell." (Matthew 10:28)

I hope that these verses instill in you the priority of heaven about how you govern your heart. But it shouldn't stop there. Practicing the lifestyle of fearlessness toward the world with the proper fear of God will allow you to see several things very clearly:

First, you will come to realize (if you haven't already) that you can be spiritual without being religious. The spirit carries weight with God, religion carries weight with people. "The mind set on the flesh is death, but the mind set on the Spirit brings life." (Romans 8:6)

You will also come to develop confidence in God's ability to save people. This is why I stopped making it my mission to "convert" anyone to the things that I thought were important. I learned that by following the Holy Spirit and being obedient to the teachings of Jesus, I could watch God save a person. I learned that it is the Holy Spirit's responsibility to bring people to himself, and not mine.

I have discovered that when I fear God there is no room in my heart to be afraid of men. When I fear God I don't care about a loss of reputation or a fear of the future. I am secure. This allows me to be non-defensive, gentle and above all, Christ-focused.

Finally, I pray that you too, can find Jesus in the eyes and heart of your Muslim friend. That you can see him as a child searching for his father and that you can take him by the hand and walk the journey of life and faith together – one step at a time.

VIII. JESUS AND JIHAD

MEETING FEAR WITH LOVE

Due to the recent acts of international terrorism in the United States, Spain, the UK, and the ongoing aggressions in the Middle East and Afghanistan, there is, understandably, a large question perched in the minds of many believers. "Is Islam safe enough to reach out to?", and "is it even worth it to make the distinction between 'American' and 'Christian' in order to maintain a sense of patriotism while at the same time being open-minded enough to accept the compassionate worldview that Jesus would have?"

This is a heavy question to consider, and many people mistakenly believe that because they are not a politician or a soldier, it is irrelevant.

A case in point: I was recently talking to a neighbor about my experiences in the Middle East. We had been working on our gardens, opposite each other, and we got to introducing ourselves. He was a deacon at his church

He asked what I did, and so I told him about my work and my friends in Lebanon. Admittedly, I gave him the best stories – who wants to make a poor impression?

"Wow," he said, leaning over the fence with his gardening gloves on and a pair of clippers in one hand, "Although I admire what you've done with your life, I can say without a doubt, I would never do anything like that."

"You never know unless you try," I said, half joking. "Seriously though, what *would* you do about your convictions versus the condition of the world?"

"You get right to the point, don't you?" He asked. He thought about it for a moment, and then said, "I'd like to say that I would *try* to reach out to Muslims, to tell them about Jesus, even to help them with their lives, you know, to be compassionate."

"Okay," I said, "but what would you *really* do? Pretend that you're in the position to make the decision."

He blew a long breath out and rubbed his chin for a moment. "I think I would squash the whole region. Cut the losses, end the debate."

"Wow," I said, "thanks for your honesty. But tell me, how can you reconcile that propensity with what you know Jesus would want you to do?"

"See, that's the catch," he said, wagging his finger at me, "it makes no difference. I'm a blue-collar worker in Denver, and the only thing I know about Islam is what I see on CNN. So, for all intents and purposes, it doesn't matter. I have my beliefs, and my convictions, but I'm not in any position to do anything about them. I'm irrelevant."

I sat up late that night, trying to read, and yet the conversation haunted me. *He can't really believe that he's irrelevant,* I thought. Then again, I could see his point. Whereas I had spent half of my life in the middle of it all, he had not. My experiences had led me to believe that what I felt in my heart toward Jesus and my Muslim friends was always immediately relevant. I couldn't talk to Jesus with bitterness or prejudice toward these people. I couldn't even talk to *them* if I was double-minded about it all.

Most American Christians are not guilty of this double-mindedness by choice. They are simply not connected to the issue in a primary sense. On the one hand, they know what they read in the Gospels to be true, but at the same time, on the other hand, they do live in a nation which has color-coded terror alerts, and they can't even take a domestic flight without wondering if it will be their last.

At the same time, a sense of insignificance to the debate has affected many people. It's not that they don't feel the call of Jesus to "love the enemy," or the statement that "love conquers all." Rather, they feel as if it is irrelevant *what* they feel or believe towards Muslims. Many people have surrendered to a sense of helplessness, believing that the only thing they can do about it all is to get out and vote. Many are so disenfranchised from politics that they don't even do that.

As a direct result, there are many followers of Jesus today who are either torn by indecision, or have given up on the whole thing because, to their existence, it is an abstraction.

My neighbor was being truthful – more than he knew. What he said in two minutes described a shadow that has fallen over many of us.

The Middle East is thousands of miles away from us, many think, *and the only thing I know about it is that some people from over there want to blow up our airplanes – with us in them.*

This isn't decadence. It isn't (at least not directly) prejudice. It's indecision, confusion, and fear; and, lacking a clear directive from God, many people feel that they "serve two masters." The one is a Jesus who was compassionate and sacrificial. The other is a sense of duty to country, to family, to religion, and to self-preservation.

Some believe that the teachings of Jesus can be, or should be, suspended during this time of national defense. Others believe that building democracies on foreign soil, or freeing oppressed people is the first item on a list of priorities. Many of my friends are military personnel, and a common phrase I hear from their collective input is: "the priority is to secure the region. Once we have removed threats and built a representative government, then we can continue with religion and social welfare."

One friend in particular, when he was frustrated by my point of view, blurted, "look, Carl – we can't tell people about Jesus if they destroy themselves or kill us. Your altruistic perspective doesn't take the human factor into account. You can't evangelize anybody when you're dying under a mushroom cloud."

I've never been in the military, so perhaps I'm missing something. However, I keep myself awake at night with the burning question, *what is the Christ-like perspective on all of this?*

I don't mean to be preachy. I actually have a strong dislike toward sanctimonious preaching. As I said in an earlier chapter: I'm a reductionist. It always, without fail, comes down to me and Jesus. I can't afford to look at my life in any other way – it would collapse around me.

So maybe I'm not complex enough. Maybe I can't see all the cards on the table. But I believe, without a doubt, that there is a question that every Christian here in the West needs to address.

What are we to do about jihad?

It becomes very difficult to "love the sinner and hate the sin," when you believe you are the target. One of my friends once said, "That's like loving the bomb and hating the explosion."

He has a point. But is it really a valid issue, or is it a way to alleviate ourselves of the cross we have tried to carry?

For many on the front lines, it is no longer an abstraction. It is a matter of clicking the safety off and shooting first, at least if they want to make it home to see their families.

This is, in every sense, a can of worms for us to consider. Myself included – I have dear friends and family on both sides of this growing conflict.

The history of war, holy or otherwise.

Much of this debate centers around an understanding (or misunderstanding) of what the roots of modern jihad are. I will give some examples - none of which I mean to be the final word. It's just data, some of it from my college days when I was slaving away for my degree, and some of it from first-hand conversations with primary sources: Muslims.

When the Ottoman Empire crumbled under the weight of European military forces, it sounded something like a death knell for much of this once-proud Islamic Empire. The Ottoman Empire was the last singular collection of Islamic nation-states, and when it fell, the last cohesive unification of Islam crumbled with it. Centuries prior to this, Islam had gone as far north as middle France, as far south as sub-Saharan Africa, and stretched from Gibraltar to Kashmir. This vast and militant empire was ruled over by a collection of Caliphs — what we could call a Caliphate or Imamate. The Caliphs were social, spiritual, political, and military leaders of their people.

After defeats in Europe, and multiple successive crusades into the holy land, Islam began to recede upon itself, diminishing mostly to the Arabian Peninsula, the Balkans, and several outlying tribal regions. It had been rebutted, and it remained so until it eventually coalesced into the Ottoman Empire in southeast Europe, down the Palestinian coastline and into Arabia and northeast Africa.

For a century or so, Islam was a mostly-collective union.

When the Ottoman Turks surrendered to impending military forces, this empire fell, relinquishing control to Catholic/Protestant Christians, and subsequently, this surrender forced the rope of the Islamic unity to unravel into warring nations, tribes, and into colonies newly owned by the various European monarchies. Once again, the "God, Gold, and Glory" of what Muslims believed to be Christendom had managed to strike into the heart of Islam. Controlling, conniving, and often corrupt, these colonial exploits often did the opposite of what Jesus had preached. "If anyone asks for your tunic, give him your shirt also." These colonial provinces did not give: they exploited.

Once again, the character of Jesus was maligned. Where traditional Islam described Jesus as a sinless prophet, what they saw instead was sinful profit. At their expense.

Fast-forward to the modern era. In the fifties, the CIA backed operations to place the Shah of Iran into power. While in the west, this was viewed as a rational act utilized in order to create a balance of power, and to offset Soviet aggression in the region, in Shi'ite Iran, it was looked at from a completely different standpoint. An intrusion of unwelcome Western influence into the only remaining Shi'a Islamic nation was neither stabilizing nor protective. With a mere glimpse at history, Muslims could see that this was simply more of the same: exploitation.

Under the Carter administration, America watched as insurgents took hostages, the Shah was forcibly displaced by the Ayatollah Khomeini, and American "stabilization" shattered. In America, this was viewed as outright hostility. To the Iranian Shi'ites, this was viewed as a reassertion of the natural order. They had recovered their nation, rejected western influence, and had a leader who could once again unite them.

In another theater, the United States sponsored, with Saudi and Pakistani help, the empowerment, training, and funding of the *mujahedin*. The freedom fighters of Afghanistan. They were the ready-and-willing buffer of Islam against the advances of Soviet expansion. America was all-too-willing to be grateful to these warriors who drove successive Soviet campaigns back north, again and again.

But now, there was a change of perspective within Islam. Instead of Islamic nations being at the "mercy" of Western influence, this time, the West relied on them. America needed the mujahedin in order to check Soviet expansion. Within the

Muslim community, pride rose, a need for recognition. A debt had been made, where was the payment?

Instead of realizing that gratitude was in order, America forgot about the Afghan and Tajik Muslims who had beaten the iron curtain. The Soviet empire fell, and with it, American reliance upon these cunning fighters dissipated.

At this point, let me ask you a question: where was Al-Queda primarily based? Afghanistan. Where was Al-Queda's financial support? Saudi Arabia. Where did Al-Queda go to build their intelligence resources? Pakistan.

America had lost it's allies from the Afghan campaign.

A band of Muslim brothers, eager for leadership, forgotten by former friends, and without a place to call their own. And thus, (this may be speculation) the Taliban was born. (*Talib* — means *defender* or *protector*).

Again we fast-forward. After years of subliminal communication between post-Soviet-threat America, and Iraq, a ruthless dictator by the name of *Saddam Hussein* decided that because the real estate of Kuwait was a historical province of Iraq, he should go and take it back for the expansion of the nation — and to add more oil fields.

And thus began Operation Desert Shield. President George HW Bush authorized military forces to deploy to the region for the sake of Kuwait, a key US ally.

From the western standpoint, this looked like a completely appropriate action. Kuwait was an ally — mostly defenseless, and Saddam Hussein was a wicked dictator who didn't bat an eye at the thought of killing thousands. An easy choice.

But the consequences, although not immediate, were severe. Saudi Arabia needed US intervention in order to ensure that Hussein's Iraqi army would not flood further south into the peninsula. Saudi Arabia gave the United States a strategic landing point from which to deploy forces: it's own territory. To the West, this seemed logical, reasonable, and perhaps even arbitrary.

To Islam it looked like this: Western Christian forces were being given access to the holiest of all lands. Saudi Arabia is the home of Mecca and Medina, the two most sacred cities in Islam. From this vantage point, these *infidels* (non-believers) were given access to attack Iraq, a secular-led nation of Muslims, and the historical site of the garden of Eden.

To the earnest Muslim, this was sacrilege, the allegiance of the US to Kuwait notwithstanding.

Meanwhile, Saudi finance continued to flow (with or without government knowledge) into the growing Taliban movement in Afghanistan and even into Pakistan.

The terror of the towers

On September eleventh, 2001, every one of us woke to the news that terrorist-controlled aircraft had crushed the tallest of American architecture in the heart of one of America's oldest and most influential cities, as well as the Pentagon, the nerve center of the US military.

Every one of us stayed glued to the television and the phone, worrying, praying, and calling relatives and friends to in order to pass on and receive news and condolences. In every sense of the word, these attacks were a massive tragedy. People jumped to their deaths to flee from the pain of the burning jet-fuel. The buildings collapsed. Thousands died. Millions mourned. The media focused in like a dart at a bulls-eye. Within hours, there were speculations about who was to blame. Within weeks there were old military contracts rebuilt within Afghanistan. Within months, the Taliban toppled.

And afterwards, the newly-paranoid American public began to seriously look into the doctrine of preemptive warfare, striking those who would harm us before they had the opportunity to do so.

And Iraq was at the top of the list, followed by Iran and North Korea. This "axis of evil" was under popular scrutiny by a nation of saddened and angered people, thousands of miles away from these locations.

How do we measure distance? If it is in the case of a ballistic nuclear missile, we tend to look at it in hours, minutes, and seconds. Precaution. ETA. Estimated Time of Arrival. We measure in megatons, we fear the size of the fallout. Threats have an urgency about them which tends to supercede all other priorities, all other considerations.

But what about the distance between us and God? While impending threats seem to overarch all other things, we have to ask ourselves these questions: are we immune? Are we protected? Are we justifiable in our military campaigns? **Does God care? Do my beliefs, actions, and inactions matter to any of this?**

This is the birthplace of my contention. Threat may loom, war may strike, and blood may be shed. But, according to the Hebrew prophet Isaiah, "the word of our God lasts forever," (Isa 40:8)

Where are we to stand, those of us who follow Jesus? I'm not talking about political distinctions. I'm referring to the conditions of our hearts. Many of us have differences: things to mourn, thoughts to reconsider, beliefs to be reexamined.

I ask only this: do not fall into the sea of those who believe that they are irrelevant. For the spiritual person, there can be no apathy. We cannot allow copouts. After all, what is the distance between us and God? Often that distance can be shortened by falling to our knees in genuine honesty. "Great are you Lord, how great is your mercy." And, "my enemies mock me, my life is at stake," and "forgive them, Father, for they do not know what they are doing."

There is deliverance and relief in the words of Jesus, There is forgiveness, compassion, and sometimes severity in his tone. It is true leadership – we would be stupid to ignore this. So why do we?

Realistically, what do we, distant as we are, foreign as we are, simple as we are, contribute to conflict with which we are the unwilling, timid, and sometimes aggressive counterparts. Why live in the shadow of inactive complacency, when we, invited by Jesus, can become what it is that we were meant to be, that which the world requires?

It is the condition of our hearts that matters most, whether we are relevant, significant, or completely disconnected. If you are not the president, are not a pastor, a soldier, a diplomat, or whatever, the condition of your heart is still as important, *for your sake*. By choosing an attitude of love and compassion toward people we don't understand, and toward an intimidatingly unknown religion, we can not only see fear and suspicion diminish, we can begin to build bridges. Bridges which lead to Jesus, the Prince of peace.

IX. APPENDIX

STATS, FACTS, AND GLOSSARY OF TERMS

Some statistics

Christianity and Islam are the two most popular religions in the world, with Christianity coming in at just over 2 billion, and Islam at 1.4 billion.

Arab countries comprise the largest demographic of Muslims at 280+ million. Sub-Saharan Africa contains 250+ million. Pakistan and Bangladesh at 230 million; and Indonesia has the highest Muslim population for an individual nation at 195 million. India and China both have 130 million Muslims, and Iran has a Shia Muslim population of 65 million. Southeast Asia has about 100 million, Soviet Central Asia and Azerbaijan have almost 50 million, and Russia has almost 30 million. Afghanistan has 23 million, whereas the United States and the European Union have only 10 million each, and Latin America has two million or less.

Glossary of terms

Allah	God (lit: *the God*)
adhan	the call to prayer
ahl-al-kitab	the people of the book; Jews and Christians
arkan-ud-din	the pillars of religion
ayatollah	a religious leader in Shia Islam
caliph	a leader of the world-wide Muslim community
dhimmi	non-Muslim in a Muslim community, a second-class citizen
fatwa	a published decree or ruling regarding theology or legislation.
hajj	the annual pilgrimage to Mecca
hadji	a person who has made the pilgrimage
hijab	the seclusion or concealment of women, also used to refer to the head-covering
Iblis	satan
imam	the leader of a mosque
iman	articles of faith
injeel	The gospels and/or the whole new testament
jihad	literally means 'struggle' and can be used to mean war. Fundamentalists generally believe this to be an additional pillar of faith
jinn	spirits

jumma	Friday, the holy day of the week
Kaba	the shrine of Mecca
mahdi	'rightly guided one', an expression used mainly by Shi'ites
mihrab	a notch in the wall of a mosque, indicating the direction of Mecca for prayers
mujahed	an Islamic warrior, *mujahedin* is plural
mullah	a religious teacher
nabi	prophet
qara	recitation, the origin of the word *Qur'an*
qibla	the direction of prayer
Qur'an	the principal holy book of Islam
Ramadan	the ninth month of the Islamic calendar, the month of the fast
salah	the daily ritual prayers
salam	peace – used in greeting
sawm	the act of fasting
shehadeh	the testimony
sharia	Islamic law
shaytan	the devil
sheikh	leader, chief
shia (or shi'ite)	a sect of Islam that believes that Ali was the rightful successor to Muhammad
shirk	the worst sin – to credit anyone to God's status
sufi	a Muslim mystic

sunni	'one of the pathway', orthodox Islam. A majority sect which believes in elected imamate.
surah	Qur'anic chapters
taqdir	predestination
tasbih	the Muslim rosary
wahabi	followers or sectarians who push puritanical reform
zabur	the psalms

SELECT BIBLIOGRAPHY

[i] Fouad Elias Accad, *Building Bridges* Navpress p. 34
[ii] Christine A. Mallouhi *Waging Peace on Islam* InterVarsity Press p. 158
[iii] Dr. Martin Luther King Jr. "How should a follower of Jesus view communism?"
[iv] Mother Teresa *In My Own Words* Gramercy Books p. 99

CARL MEDEARIS is an internationally known speaker on such issues as pan Islamic/Christian relationships and international bridge-building between the East and the West. He lives in Denver, Colorado with his wife and three children. For more information or for additional copies of this work, please e-mail Carl at: *carl.medearis@nowmail.org*

PHILLIP STROPLE is a freelance writer and editor. He currently works as a staff writer/editor for several religious/geopolitical organizations as well as a writing consultant for other authors. He lives in Colorado Springs, Colorado with his wife and three children. For correspondence, please contact Phillip at: *deosynthetic@hotmail.com*

COVER CREDITS: Cover photo and design by Aaron Luttrell of RedApollo design: *aaron@aaronluttrell.com*